Kaplan Publishing are constantly finding new ways to support students looking for exam success and our online resources really do add an extra dimension to your studies.

This book comes with free MyKaplan online resources so that you can study anytime, anywhere. **This free online resource is not sold separately and is included in the price of the book.**

Having purchased this book, you have access to the following online study materia

CONTENT	AAT	
	Text	Kit
Electronic version of the book	✓	✓
Knowledge Check tests with instant answers	✓	
Mock assessments online	✓	✓
Material updates	✓	✓

How to access your online resources

Received this book as part of your Kaplan course?
If you have a MyKaplan account, your full online resources will be added automatically, in line with the information in your course confirmation email. If you've not used MyKaplan before, you'll be sent an activation email once your resources are ready.

Bought your book from Kaplan?
We'll automatically add your online resources to your MyKaplan account. If you've not used MyKaplan before, you'll be sent an activation email.

Bought your book from elsewhere?
Go to **www.mykaplan.co.uk/add-online-resources**
Enter the ISBN number found on the title page and back cover of this book.
Add the unique pass key number contained in the scratch panel below.
You may be required to enter additional information during this process to set up or confirm your account details.

This code can only be used once for the registration of this book online. This registration and your online content will expire when the examinations covered by this book have taken place. Please allow one hour from the time you submit your book details for us to process your request.

Please scratch the film to access your unique code.

Please be aware that this code is case-sensitive and you will need to include the dashes within the passcode, but not when entering the ISBN.

AAT

Q2022

Cash and Financial Management

EXAM KIT

This Study Text supports study for the following AAT qualifications:

AAT Level 4 Diploma in Professional Accounting

AAT Diploma in Professional Accounting at SCQF Level 8

AAT: CASH AND FINANCIAL MANAGEMENT

British Library Cataloguing-in-Publication Data

A catalogue record for this book is available from the British Library.

Published by:

Kaplan Publishing UK
Unit 2 The Business Centre
Molly Millar's Lane
Wokingham
Berkshire
RG41 2QZ

ISBN: 978-1-83996-899-0

© Kaplan Financial Limited, 2024

Printed and bound in Great Britain.

The text in this material and any others made available by any Kaplan Group company does not amount to advice on a particular matter and should not be taken as such. No reliance should be placed on the content as the basis for any investment or other decision or in connection with any advice given to third parties. Please consult your appropriate professional adviser as necessary. Kaplan Publishing Limited and all other Kaplan group companies expressly disclaim all liability to any person in respect of any losses or other claims, whether direct, indirect, incidental, consequential or otherwise arising in relation to the use of such materials.

All rights reserved. No part of this examination may be reproduced or transmitted in any form or by any means, electronic or mechanical, including photocopying, recording, or by any information storage and retrieval system, without prior permission from Kaplan Publishing.

This Product includes content from the International Auditing and Assurance Standards Board (IAASB) and the International Ethics Standards Board for Accountants (IESBA), published by the International Federation of Accountants (IFAC) in 2015 and is used with permission of IFAC.

CONTENTS

	Page
Unit-specific information	P.4
Index to questions and answers	P.5
Exam technique	P.6
Kaplan's recommended revision approach	P.7

Practice questions	1
Answers to practice questions	77
Mock assessment questions	143
Answers to mock assessment questions	157

> **Features in this exam kit**
>
> In addition to providing a wide ranging bank of real assessment style questions, we have also included in this kit:
>
> • unit-specific information and advice on assessment technique
>
> • our recommended approach to make your revision for this particular subject as effective as possible.

You will find a wealth of other resources to help you with your studies on the AAT website:

www.aat.org.uk/

Quality and accuracy are of the utmost importance to us so if you spot an error in any of our products, please send an email to mykaplanreporting@kaplan.com with full details, or follow the link to the feedback form in MyKaplan.

Our Quality Co-ordinator will work with our technical team to verify the error and take action to ensure it is corrected in future editions.

UNIT-SPECIFIC INFORMATION

THE EXAM

FORMAT OF THE ASSESSMENT

The assessment is divided into several standalone tasks which cover all of the learning outcomes and assessment criteria. Some of the tasks are extended writing tasks and will be marked by a human.

In any one assessment, students may not be assessed on all content, or on the full depth or breadth of a piece of content. The content assessed may change over time to ensure validity of assessment, but all assessment criteria will be tested over time.

The learning outcomes for this unit are as follows:

	Learning outcome	Weighting
1	Prepare forecasts for cash receipts and payments	15%
2	Prepare cash budgets and monitor cash flows	25%
3	Understand the importance of managing finance and liquidity	15%
4	Understand ways of raising finance and investing funds	20%
5	Understand regulations and organisational policies that influence decisions in managing cash and finance	25%
	Total	100%

Time allowed

2 hours

PASS MARK

The pass mark for all AAT CBAs is 70%.

 Always keep your eye on the clock and make sure you attempt all questions!

DETAILED SYLLABUS

The detailed syllabus and study guide written by the AAT can be found at:

www.aat.org.uk/

INDEX TO QUESTIONS AND ANSWERS

		Page number	
		Question	Answer
CASH AND PROFIT			
1	Types of cash flow	1	77
2 – 15	Cash adjustments	2	77
FORECASTING			
16 – 20	Moving averages	14	85
21 – 23	Mark-up and margin	17	88
24 – 29	Indexing	18	89
30 – 36	Regression analysis	21	90
PREPARING CASH BUDGETS			
37 – 46	Cash receipts	24	92
47 – 58	Cash payments	28	95
59 – 65	Cash budgets	34	100
ANALYSING AND MONITORING CASH BUDGETS			
66 – 77	Sensitivity analysis	41	106
78 – 82	Monitoring cash budgets	50	113
LIQUIDITY MANAGEMENT			
83 – 99	Liquidity and working capital	54	117
RAISING FINANCE			
100 – 104	Interest rates	58	120
105 – 130	Financing options	59	120
INVESTING SURPLUS FUNDS			
131 – 155		68	131
IMPACT OF REGULATIONS AND POLICIES ON FINANCING AND INVESTMENT			
156 – 162	Government policy and regulations	74	141

MOCK ASSESSMENT		
Questions and answers	143	157

KAPLAN PUBLISHING

EXAM TECHNIQUE

- **Do not skip any of the material** in the syllabus.
- **Read each question** *very* carefully.
- **Double-check your answer** before committing yourself to it.
- Answer **every** question – if you do not know an answer to a multiple choice question or true/false question, you don't lose anything by guessing. Think carefully before you **guess**.
- If you are answering a multiple-choice question, **eliminate first those answers that you know are wrong**. Then choose the most appropriate answer from those that are left.
- **Don't panic** if you realise you've answered a question incorrectly. Getting one question wrong will not mean the difference between passing and failing

Computer-based assessments – tips

- Do not attempt a CBA until you have **completed all study material** relating to it.
- On the AAT website there is a CBA demonstration. It is **ESSENTIAL** that you attempt this before your real CBA. You will become familiar with how to move around the CBA screens and the way that questions are formatted, increasing your confidence and speed in the actual assessment.
- Be sure you understand how to use the **software** before you start the assessment. If in doubt, ask the assessment centre staff to explain it to you.
- Questions are **displayed on the screen** and answers are entered using keyboard and mouse. At the end of the assessment, you are given a certificate showing the result you have achieved.
- In addition to the traditional multiple-choice question type, CBAs will also contain **other types of questions**, such as number entry questions, drag and drop, true/false, pick lists or drop down menus or hybrids of these.
- In some CBAs you will have to type in written answers.
- You need to be sure you **know how to answer questions** of this type before you sit the assessment, through practice.

KAPLAN'S RECOMMENDED REVISION APPROACH

QUESTION PRACTICE IS THE KEY TO SUCCESS

Success in professional assessments relies upon you acquiring a firm grasp of the required knowledge at the tuition phase. In order to be able to do the questions, knowledge is essential.

However, the difference between success and failure often hinges on your assessment technique on the day and making the most of the revision phase of your studies.

The **Kaplan textbook** is the starting point, designed to provide the underpinning knowledge to tackle all questions. However, in the revision phase, poring over text books is not the answer.

Kaplan pocket notes are designed to help you quickly revise a topic area; however you then need to practise questions. There is a need to progress to assessment style questions as soon as possible, and to tie your assessment technique and technical knowledge together.

The importance of question practice cannot be over-emphasised.

The recommended approach below is designed by expert tutors in the field, in conjunction with their knowledge of the examiner and the specimen assessment.

You need to practise as many questions as possible in the time you have left.

OUR AIM

Our aim is to get you to the stage where you can attempt assessment questions confidently, to time, in a closed book environment, with no supplementary help (i.e. to simulate the real assessment experience).

Practising your assessment technique is also vitally important for you to assess your progress and identify areas of weakness that may need more attention in the final run up to the assessment.

In order to achieve this we recognise that initially you may feel the need to practise some questions with open book help.

Good assessment technique is vital.

THE KAPLAN REVISION PLAN

Stage 1: Assess areas of strengths and weaknesses

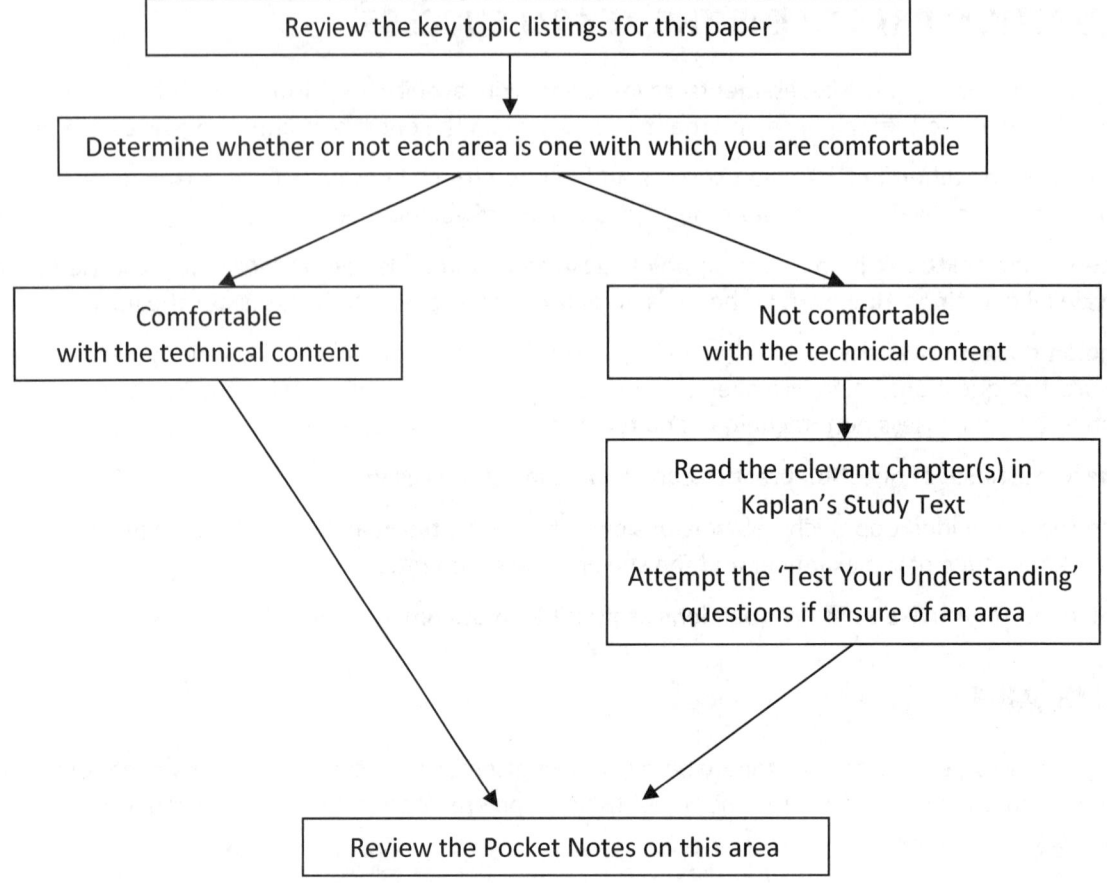

Stage 2: Practice questions

Follow the order of revision of topics as presented in this kit and attempt the questions in the order suggested.

Try to avoid referring to text books and notes and the model answer until you have completed your attempt.

Review your attempt with the model answer and assess how much of the answer you achieved.

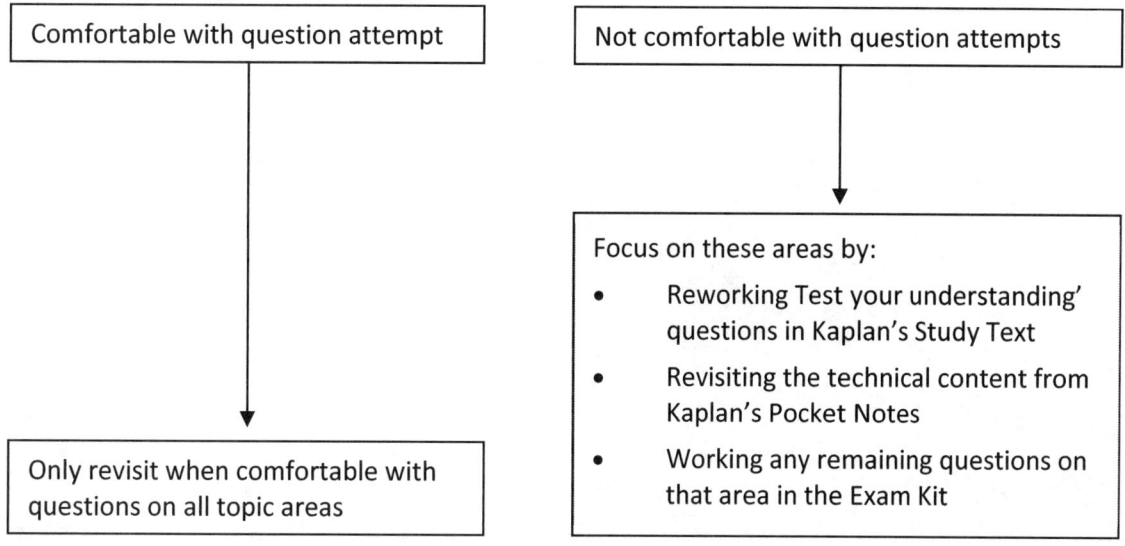

Stage 3: Final pre-assessment revision

We recommend that you **attempt at least one two and a half hour mock assessment** containing a set of previously unseen assessment standard questions.

Attempt the mock CBA online in timed, closed book conditions to simulate the real exam experience.

Section 1

PRACTICE QUESTIONS

CASH AND PROFIT

TYPES OF CASH FLOW

1   Complete the table by selecting the best description from the list of options below to match the type of cash receipt or cash payment.

Description	Type of receipt or payment
Proceeds from the disposal of non-current assets	
Buy new factory	
Customer paying their debt	
Pay legal fee due to product complaints	
Unexpected tax refund	
Payment of wages	
Pay corporation tax for the year	
Payments made to the owners of the business	

Options

1   Capital payment

2   Capital receipts

3   Drawings

4   Exceptional payment

5   Exceptional receipt

6   Regular revenue receipt

7   Regular revenue expense

8   Payment to HM Revenue and Customs

AAT: CASH AND FINANCIAL MANAGEMENT

CASH ADJUSTMENTS

2 Statement of Financial Position extract:

Balances as at:	31 October 20X8	31 October 20X9
	£	£
Trade receivables	10,500	12,900
Prepayment – rent	750	1,000
Accrual – payroll expenses	200	320
Trade payables	5,800	6,300

Statement of profit or loss extract for the year ended 31 October 20X9

	£	£
Revenue		300,000
Less: Purchases		(150,000)
Gross profit		150,000
Less: Expenses		
Payroll	22,120	
Rent	6,000	
Utilities	10,000	
		(38,120)
		111,880

(a) Prepare the trade receivables account, showing clearly the cash received from receivables in the year.

Trade receivables

	£		£

(b) Prepare the rent account, showing clearly the amount of cash paid for rent for the year.

Rent

	£		£

(c) Prepare the payroll expenses account, showing clearly the cash paid for payroll expenses for the year.

Payroll expenses

£	£

(d) Prepare the trade payables account, showing clearly the cash paid to the payables in the year.

Trade payables

£	£

3   The following items were extracted from a company's budget for next month:

	£
Purchases on credit	360,000
Expected decrease in inventory during the month	12,000
Expected increase in trade payables during the month	15,000

What is the budgeted payment to trade payables for the month?

A   £333,000

B   £345,000

C   £357,000

D   £375,000

4   DY had a balance outstanding on trade receivables at 30 April 20X6 of £70,000. Forecast credit sales for the next six months are £200,000 and customers are expected to return goods with a sales value of £2,000.

Based on past experience, within the next six months DY expects to collect £250,000 cash and to write off as irrecoverable debts 3% of the balance outstanding at 30 April 20X6.

Calculate DY's forecast trade receivables outstanding at 31 October 20X6.

AAT: CASH AND FINANCIAL MANAGEMENT

5 (a) The following items are included in a company's budget for next month:

	£
Sales on credit	240,000
Expected increase in inventory next month	20,000
Expected decrease in trade receivables next month	12,000

What is the budgeted receipt from trade receivables next month?

(b) **Identify whether the following items affect cash, profit, or both cash and profit.**

Item	Cash	Profit	Cash and profit
Depreciation			
Selling a non-current asset for its carry value			
Repaying a loan			
Prepaying next year's rent			
Making a cash sale			

6 A business disposed of a number of non-current assets.

Calculate the cash received in each of the following situations.

(a) A vehicle has been disposed of during the year.

- The original cost of the vehicle was £12,000.
- The accumulated depreciation on the vehicle was £5,250.
- The loss on disposal was £1,750.

How much cash was received?

(b) An item of equipment was disposed of during the year.

- The original cost of the equipment was £500.
- It was purchased 3 years ago and depreciation is provided at 20% on a straight line basis.
- There was a gain of £75 from the sale of this equipment.

How much cash was received?

(c) A vehicle was part-exchanged for a new one during the year.

- The original cost of the vehicle which was part-exchanged was £12,000.
- The carrying amount of the vehicle which was part-exchanged was £6,144.
- The part exchange would generate a book loss on the old car of £2,644.
- The new vehicle's total cost was £13,500.

What was the value of the part-exchange and therefore how much cash was spent buying the new vehicle?

7 Haul Punt owns a business which caters for weddings and other grand functions. Haul prepares quarterly statements of profit or loss and statements of financial position. These are prepared on an accruals basis.

Haul likes to use the freshest ingredients, so these are mainly purchased when required and therefore very little inventory is maintained. All sales and purchases are made on credit terms.

The statement of profit or loss for Haul's business for the quarter ended June is as follows:

	£	£
Revenue		51,000
Less: Purchases		(26,000)
Gross profit		25,000
Less: Expenses		
Wages	12,900	
Advertising expenses	2,010	
Van expenses	3,069	
Van depreciation	2,567	
		(20,546)
		4,454

Extracts from the statement of financial position at 1 April and 30 June show the following:

Statement of financial position at	1 April	30 June
	£	£
Receivables	3,520	12,400
Payables	400	3,004
Accruals – advertising	1,200	800
Prepayments – van expenses	80	110

Calculate the actual business cash receipts and cash payments for the quarter to 30 June.

	£
Sales receipts	
Purchases payments	
Wages paid	
Advertising fees paid	
Van expenses	
Van depreciation	

8 The statement of profit or loss for Ben's business for the quarter ended June shows the following:

	£
Revenue	351,000
Purchases	126,000
Wages expense	32,900
Electricity expenses	22,010
Van expenses	23,069
Phone expense	12,567

Extracts from the statements of financial position at 1 April and 30 June show the following:

Statement of financial position at	1 April	30 June
	£	£
Receivables	13,520	31,000
Payables	4,400	8,000
Accruals – electricity and van	1,200	2,100
Prepayments – phone expenses	80	–

Calculate the actual business cash receipts and cash payments for the quarter to 30 June.

	£
Sales receipts	
Purchases payments	
Wages paid	
Electricity and van expenses paid	
Phone expenses	

9 S Nynan owns a wedding stationery business and prepares quarterly statements of profit or loss and statements of financial positions. These are prepared on an accruals basis.

Stationery materials are purchased when required and therefore very little inventory is maintained. All sales and purchases are made on credit terms.

The following information has been extracted from the accounting information for S Nynan's business for the quarter ended September:

	Statement of profit or loss £	Opening position Prepayments £	Opening position Accruals £	Closing position Prepayments £	Closing position Accruals £
Rent	12,650	1,200			1,200
Office expenses	6,640		370		441
Printing expenses	17,118	3,655		567	

Calculate the actual business cash payments for the quarter ended September.

	£
Rent paid	
Office expenses paid	
Printing expenses paid	

10 Riko started trading on 1 April 20X6. She is a computer technician working for small businesses and all trade is on credit.

Extracts from the statement of profit or loss as at 31 March 20X7:

	£
Revenue	29,200
Purchases	11,200
Rent	3,600
General expenses	1,840

- On 31 March 20X7, trade receivables owed £3,400.
- On 31 March 20X7, £1,195 was owed to payables for supplies.
- Discounts were received amounting to £1,165.
- The cash paid for rent included a payment of £900 for rent of the premises for the period 1 April 20X7 to 30 June 20X7.
- During May 20X7, a payment of £135 was made for electricity used during the period 1 February 20X7 to 30 April 20X7. Electricity is charged to general expenses.

(a) Calculate the cash received from receivables for the year ended 31 March 20X7

(b) Calculate the cash paid to payables for the year ended 31 March 20X7

(c) Calculate the cash paid for rent for the year ended 31 March 20X7

(d) Calculate the cash paid for general expenses for the year ended 31 March 20X7

11 The following forecast information has been provided for a business for the quarter ending 31 July 20X6:

	£	£
Revenue		15,000
Less: Cost of sales		
Opening inventory	1,200	
Purchases	2,400	
Closing inventory	(1,000)	
		(2,600)
Gross profit		12,400
Expenses		1,880
Operating profit		10,520
Tax		2,700
Profit after tax		7,820

AAT: CASH AND FINANCIAL MANAGEMENT

Additional information

1. The company believes that 15% of total sales will be cash sales and the rest will be on credit. The balance of trade receivables at 1 May 20X6 was £10,000 and the company expects trade receivables at the end of July 20X6 will be 60% of the credit sales for the quarter.

2. All purchases are to be made on credit terms. The balance of trade payables at 1 May 20X6 was £1,200. Total payments for purchases during the quarter will be £2,000.

3. Expenses include a depreciation charge of £250. All other expenses are settled on cash terms.

4. The carrying value of the non-current assets at 1 May 20X6 was £20,000 and the carrying value at 31 July 20X6 is forecast to be £24,000. The company will pay for any additions immediately by cash.

5. The tax payable shown in the statement of financial position was £2,600 at 1 May 20X6 and is expected to be £2,800 at 31 July 20X6

6. The cash position at 1 May 20X6 was £30,000.

Calculate the closing cash position at 31 July 20X6. Use brackets or minus signs where appropriate.

	£
Operating profit	
Change in inventory	
Change in receivables	
Change in payables	
Adjustment for non-cash items	
Purchase of non-current assets	
Tax paid	
Net change in cash position	
Cash position 1 May 20X6	
Forecast cash position 31 July 20X6	

12 The following forecast information has been provided for a business for the next year 20X6:

	£	£
Revenue		600,000
Less: Cost of sales		
Opening inventory	50,000	
Purchases	200,000	
Closing inventory	(50,000)	
		(200,000)
Gross profit		400,000
Expenses		(150,000)
Operating profit		250,000
Tax		(52,500)
Profit after tax		197,500

Additional information

1   The company believes that 90% of total sales will be credit sales and the rest will be cash. The balance of trade receivables at 1 January 20X6 was £100,000 and the company expects trade receivables at the end of December 20X6 to be 20% of the credit sales for the year.

2   All purchases are to be made on credit terms. The balance of trade payables at 1 January 20X6 was £50,000. Total payments for purchases during the year will be £230,000.

3   Expenses include a depreciation charge of £25,000. All other expenses are settled on cash terms.

4   The carrying value of the non-current assets at 1 January 20X6 was £20,000 and the carrying value at 31 December 20X6 is forecast to be £24,000. In March 20X6 the business will take out a new long term lease to acquire a new machine that would otherwise cost £15,000. The lease is repayable at £625 per month.

5   The tax payable shown in the statement of financial position was £50,000 at 1 January 20X6 and is expected to be £55,000 at 31 December 20X6

6   The forecast cash position at 1 January 20X6 was £70,000 in hand

Calculate the closing cash position at 31 December 20X6. Use brackets or minus signs where appropriate.

	£
Operating profit	
Change in inventory	
Change in receivables	
Change in payables	
Adjustment for non-cash items	
Purchase of non-current assets	
Tax paid	
Net change in cash position	
Cash position 1 January 20X6	
Forecast cash position 31 December 20X6	

13 Style Limited is a clothing manufacturer. Extracts from the trial balance at 31 March 20X5 for Style Limited's were as follows:

	£000	£000
6% loan notes (redeemable 20Y0)		1,500
Administrative expenses	1,540	
Cash and cash equivalents	822	
Cost of sales	3,463	
Distribution costs	1,590	
Inventory at 31 March 20X5	1,320	
Land and buildings at cost at 31 March 20X4	5,190	
Plant and equipment at cost at 31 March 20X4	3,400	
Accumulated depreciation at 31 March 20X4: Buildings		1,500
Accumulated depreciation at 31 March 20X4: Plant and equipment		1,659
Revenue		8,210

Additional information provided:

(i)   There were no sales or purchases of non-current assets or available for sale investments during the year ended 31 March 20X5.

(ii) Income tax due for the year ended 31 March 20X5 is estimated at £250,000. There is no balance outstanding in relation to previous years' corporate income tax. The deferred tax provision needs to be increased by £100,000.

(iii) Depreciation is charged on buildings using the straight-line basis at 3% each year. The cost of land included in land and buildings is £2,000,000. Plant and equipment is depreciated using the reducing balance method at 20%. Depreciation is regarded as a cost of sales.

(iv) Style Limited entered into a 9 month lease on 1 November 20X4 to acquire machinery to manufacture a bespoke range of kitchen units for a one off customer. The lease payments consist of a £18,000 deposit, then £4000 each month in arrears. The machine is estimated to have a useful economic life of 20 years.

(v)   The 6% loan notes are 10 year loans due for repayment March 20Y0. Style Limited incurred no other finance costs in the year to 31 March 20X5.

Prepare the statement of profit or loss for Style Limited for the year to 31 March 20X5.

Style Limited's statement of profit or loss for the year ended 31 March 20X5

	£000
Revenue	
Cost of sales	_____
Gross profit	
Administrative expenses	
Distribution costs	_____
Operating profit	
Finance cost	_____
Profit before tax	
Income tax expense	_____
Profit for the period	

14 The accounting books of Ruby and Daughters are incomplete, however it was possible to find out the following information.

The 20X5 accounts showed the following closing balances:

Non-current assets	£50,000
Inventory	£5,000
Receivables	£12,000
Cash at bank	£33,000
Cash in hand	£2,000
Payables	£7,000

The cash account at the end of 20X6 showed the following:

Cash account

	£		£
Balance b/d	2,000	Bankings	38,000
Cash from customers	40,000	Wages	800
		Sundry expenses	200
		Balance c/d	3,000
	_____		_____
	42,000		42,000
	_____		_____

The bank account at the end of 20X6 showed the following:

Bank account

	£		£
Balance b/d	33,000	Salaries	20,000
Bankings from cash	38,000	Rent	5,000
		Credit purchases	25,000
		Drawings	10,000
		Balance c/d	11,000
	71,000		71,000

A review of outstanding sales invoices, unpaid at the year-end showed a total of £16,000.

Ruby says that the business currently owes about £5,000 for building materials.

Inventory levels have increased by 20% from the start of the year.

At year-end there is a sundry expense accrual of £50 and a rent prepayment of £300.

Depreciation is to be provided at 20% on carrying value.

Prepare a statement of profit or loss for the year 20X6.

Ruby and Daughters

Statement of profit or loss for the year

	£	£
Sales		
Opening inventory		
Purchases		
Less: Closing inventory		
Cost of sales		
Gross profit		
Less:		
Wages and salaries		
Rent		
Sundry expenses		
Depreciation		
Net profit/(loss)		

15 The following extracts from the financial statements are available:

Extracts from the budget statement of financial position	Period 3 £000	Period 4 £000
NBV Non-current assets	930	858
Trade receivables	445	423
Car lease payable	(6)	(5)
Cash	13	15
Trade payables	(435)	(433)

Extracts from the budgeted income statement	Period 3 £000	Period 4 £000
Turnover	720	760
Purchases	(718)	(427)
Other expenses	(110)	(126)
Car leasing	(12)	(13)
Depreciation	(65)	(60)
Loss on disposal of a non-current asset	–	(3)

Additional information

1 Cash sales represent 10% of turnover

2 The receipt from the disposal of the non-current asset occurs in the same period the disposal is made

3 The car lease qualifies as a short term lease and is expensed to the statement of profit and loss over the length of the lease.

Using the information above, complete the period 4 extract of the cash budget. Use minus signs where appropriate.

Extract of the cash budget	Period 4 £000
Receipts of cash sales	76
Receipts from trade receivables	706
Receipt from disposal of non-current asset	9
Car lease payments	(14)

AAT: CASH AND FINANCIAL MANAGEMENT

FORECASTING

MOVING AVERAGES

16 A company is preparing its forecast sales and purchase information for January.

The sales volume trend is to be identified using a 3–point moving average based on the actual monthly sales volume.

(a) Complete the table below to calculate the current monthly sales volume trend and identify any monthly variations using the additive model.

	Sales volume (units)	Trend	Monthly variation
May	61,600		
June	39,100		
July	55,300		
August	72,100		
September	49,600		
October	65,800		
November	82,600		
December	60,100		

Additional information

The selling price per unit has been set at £14.50.

Monthly purchases are estimated to be 30% of the value of the forecast sales.

(b) Using the trend and the monthly variations identified in part (a) complete the table below to forecast the sales volume, sales value and purchase value for January of the next financial year.

	Forecast trend	Variation	Forecast sales volume	Forecast sales £	Forecast purchases £
January					

17 A company is preparing its forecast sales and purchase information for December.

The sales volume trend is to be identified using a 5–point moving average based on the actual monthly sales volumes.

(a) Complete the table below to calculate the current monthly sales volume trend and identify any monthly variations using the additive model.

	Sales volume (units)	Trend	Monthly variation
January	19,906		
February	22,390		
March	20,555	20,570	−15
April	18,666	20,620	−1,954
May	21,333	20,670	663
June	20,156	20,720	−564
July	22,640	20,770	1,870
August	20,805	20,820	−15
September	18,916	20,870	−1,954
October	21,583		
November	20,406		

Additional information

The selling price per unit has been set at £30.

Monthly purchases are estimated to be 28% of the value of the forecast sales.

(b) Using the trend and the monthly variations identified in part (a) calculate the forecast purchases value for December.

	Forecast purchases £
December	192,276

18 A company is preparing its forecast sales and purchase information.

The sales volume trend is to be identified using a 3–point moving average based on the actual monthly sales volumes.

(a) Complete the table below to calculate the current monthly sales volume trend and identify any monthly variations using the multiplicative model.

	Sales volume (units)	Trend	Monthly variation (2 dp)
October	6,408		
November	8,816	8,303	1.06
December	9,686	8,479	1.14
January	6,934	8,713	0.80
February	9,520	8,965	1.06
March	10,440	9,140	1.14
April	7,460	9,375	0.80
May	10,225		

(b) The average monthly trend (to the nearest whole number) is **214**

AAT: CASH AND FINANCIAL MANAGEMENT

19 **(a)** Which of the following are illustrations of a seasonal variation? (Tick two)

Sales of footballs increase when the world cup is on.	
Sales of greetings cards increase in December.	
Sales of milk remain constant all year.	
Sales of houses increase in Spring.	
Sales of newspapers rise whenever it rains.	

(b) Which of the following is an illustration of a cyclical variation? (Tick one)

Tennis rackets sales increase during Wimbledon.	
Over summer, more hosepipes are sold.	
Sales of raincoats increase in April.	
During the last general election, sales of ice-cream increased.	
Sales of diet books reach a peak after every Olympics.	

(c) Complete the sentences below by picking the correct options.

A seasonal variation is a change in sales which occurs **[at regular intervals, normally of less than a year/at random/regularly but not every year]** whereas a cyclical variation occurs **[at the same time every year/at random/over a long time period]**.

The underlying sales trend is the sales level excluding **[seasonal variation/random variation/cyclical variation/all variations]**.

20 **(a)** Which of the following are illustrations of a seasonal variation? (Tick two)

Sales of houses increase when the England cricket team wins.	
Sales of wrapping paper increase in November and December.	
Sales of venetian blinds have been falling consistently for 3 years.	
Sales of wallpaper increase at the same time that sales of toothpaste fall.	
Sales of shoes rise in summer.	

(b) Which of the following is an illustration of a cyclical variation? (Tick one)

Tennis rackets sales decrease when it rains.	
Over summer, more ice creams are sold.	
Sales of gloves increase in Autumn.	
When Sky HD was launched a carpet firm in Cardiff experienced 20% sales growth.	
Over the last 50 years the average price of oil has increased for 5 years, then decreased for 5 years. This pattern continued over the 50 year period.	

MARK-UP AND MARGIN

21 If purchases are £900 (assuming purchases are the only component of the cost of sales)

(a) What would sales be if a 40% mark-up was applied?

(b) What would the sales be if the sales margin was 40%?

22 A company is preparing its forecast sales and purchase information for October.

The sales volume trend is to be identified using a 3–point moving average based on the actual monthly sales volumes.

(a) Complete the table below to calculate the current monthly sales volume trend and identify any monthly variations using the additive model.

	Sales volume (units)	Trend	Monthly variation
February	10,100		
March	10,950		
April	11,650		
May	11,000		
June	11,850		
July	12,550		
August	11,900		
September	12,750		

The monthly variation in July is _____ units.

Additional information

The selling price per unit has been set at £21.50.

(b) Using the trend and the monthly variations identified in part (a) complete the table below to forecast the sales volume and sales value for October.

	Forecast trend	Variation	Forecast sales volume	Forecast sales £
October				

(c) If the company has a margin of 20%, assuming that purchases are the only component of the cost of sales, the value of the purchases will be £ _____.

(d) If the company adds a mark-up of 25%, assuming that purchases are the only component of the cost of sales, the value of the purchases will be £ _____.

AAT: CASH AND FINANCIAL MANAGEMENT

23 Salah Limited is a manufacturing company, specialising in a single product, the 'Benji'. The company's yearend is 31 December.

The company is organised in two divisions: Manufacturing and Sales.

When goods are completed they are transferred from Manufacturing to Sales at full production cost plus a 5% mark up.

The Sales division is then responsible for onward sale to external customers. The Sales department applies a 10% mark up to calculate the selling price.

A few sales to external customers (with a 7% margin applied) are made by the Manufacturing division directly (i.e. without going through Sales).

The table below contains the total purchase costs of the units sold in the first 3 months of 20X0.

	Manufacturing Division		
	To external customers	To Sales Division	Total
	£	£	£
20X0			
January	51	230	281
February	60	140	200
March	18	132	150

Calculate the value of the total monthly sales value to external customers for the first 3 months of 20X0 (round to the nearest penny).

INDEXING

24 The price of biscuits is set on the first day of every month. The price for the last four months is given below.

Create an index for the price of biscuits using month 3 as the base period.

Month	1	2	3	4	5	6	7
Price	0.12	0.15	0.21	0.32	0.26	0.25	0.30
Index							

25 The company uses an industry wage rate index to forecast future monthly wage costs. Employees receive a pay increase in October each year. The monthly wage cost of £20,500 was calculated when the wage index was 131.

The forecast wage rate index for the next three months is:

August 142
September 146
October 151

If the company uses the forecast wage rate index, what will the wage cost for October be, to the nearest £?

A £30,955

B £20,651

C £23,630

D £22,899

26 Four years ago material X cost £5 per kg and the price index most appropriate to the cost of material X stood at 150. The same index now stands at 430.

What is the best estimate of the current cost of material X per kg?

A £1.74

B £9.33

C £14.33

D £21.50

27 Two years ago the price index appropriate to the cost of material Y had a value of 120. It now has a value of 160.

If material Y costs £2,000 per kg today, what would the cost per kg have been two years ago?

A £1,500

B £1,667

C £2,667

D £3,200

28 (a) **Using the following information calculate the missing figures for the sales price (to 2 decimal places) and index, using the information for Period 1 as a base.**

Period	1	2	3	4	5
Sales price £	40.00	55.00		48.00	
Index	80.00		120.00		121.00

(b) **If the company was making a margin of 20% on the sales price, what was the cost price in period 1?**

£

AAT: CASH AND FINANCIAL MANAGEMENT

29 A company has its own temperature-regulated greenhouses to enable year round growing of herbs and other ingredients. They are preparing the forecast purchases of manure (in tonnes) for next year. The sales volume trend is to be identified using a 3-month moving average.

(a) Complete the table below, calculate the monthly purchases volume trend and identify any monthly variations. Enter minus signs where appropriate, and round to the nearest whole number.

Month	Purchases volume (tonnes)	Trend	Monthly variation
1	5,150		
2	5,241		
3	5,487		
4	5,615		
5	5,280		
6	5,456		
7	5,648		
8	5,890		
9	5,448		
10	5,689		
11	5,847		
12	6,000		

(b) Calculate the average monthly trend to the nearest whole number.

(c) Calculate the forecast purchases trend for month 17 and 18.

Month 17 (tonnes)	Month 18 (tonnes)

The purchase price per tonne in month 7 was £56 when the cost index was 125. The cost index for month 18 is expected to be 142.

(d) Calculate the purchase cost for month 18

REGRESSION ANALYSIS

30 The overhead costs of RP have been found to be represented by the formula:

$$y = £10,000 + £0.25x$$

where y is the monthly cost and x represents the activity level measured as the number of orders.

Monthly activity levels of orders may be estimated using a combined regression analysis and time series model:

$$a = 100,000 + 30b$$

where a represents the de-seasonalised monthly activity level and b represents the month number.

In month 240, the seasonal index value is 108.

Calculate the overhead cost for RP for month 240 to the nearest £1,000.

31 Z plc has found that it can estimate future sales using time series analysis and regression techniques. The following trend equation has been derived:

$$y = 25,000 + 6,500x$$

where

y is the total sales units per quarter

x is the time period reference number

Z has also derived the following set of seasonal variation index values for each quarter using a multiplicative model:

Quarter 1	70
Quarter 2	90
Quarter 3	150
Quarter 4	90

Using the above model, calculate the forecast for sales units for the third quarter of year 7, assuming that the first quarter of year 1 is time period reference number 1.

AAT: CASH AND FINANCIAL MANAGEMENT

The following data relate to Questions 32 and 33.

H is forecasting its sales for next year using a combination of time series and regression analysis models. An analysis of past sales units has produced the following equation for the quarterly sales trend:

$$y = 26x + 8{,}850$$

where the value of x represents the quarterly accounting period and the value of y represents the quarterly sales trend in units. Quarter 1 of next year will have a value for x of 25.

The quarterly seasonal variations have been measured using the multiplicative (proportional) model and are:

Quarter 1   – 15%
Quarter 2   – 5%
Quarter 3   + 5%
Quarter 4   + 15%

Production is planned to occur at a constant rate throughout the year.

The company does not hold inventories at the end of any year.

32 The difference between the budgeted sales for quarter 1 and quarter 4 next year are:

    A   78 units

    B   2,850 units

    C   2,862 units

    D   2,940 units

33 The number of units to be produced in each quarter of next year will be nearest to:

    A   9,454 units

    B   9,493 units

    C   9,532 units

    D   9,543 units

34 A company is preparing its annual budget and is estimating the number of units of Product A that it will sell in each quarter of Year 2. Past experience has shown that the trend for sales of the product is represented by the following relationship:

y = a + bx where

y = number of sales units in the quarter

a = 10,000 units

b = 3,000 units

x = the quarter number where 1 = quarter 1 of Year 1

Actual sales of Product A in Year 1 were affected by seasonal variations and were as follows:

Quarter 1:	14,000 units
Quarter 2:	18,000 units
Quarter 3:	18,000 units
Quarter 4:	20,000 units

Calculate the expected sales of Product A (in units) for each quarter of Year 2, after adjusting for seasonal variations using the additive model.

35 Production overhead costs at company BW are assumed to vary with the number of machine hours worked. A line of best fit will be calculated from the following historical data, with costs adjusted to allow for cost inflation over time.

Year	Total production Overheads £	Number of machine hours	Cost index
20X8	143,040	3,000	192
20X9	156,000	3,200	200
20Y0	152,320	2,700	224
20Y1	172,000	3,000	235

(a) **Restate the cost data at the 20Y1 price level, to remove differences caused by inflation.**

If the line of best fit, based on current (20Y1) prices, is calculated as:

y = 33,000 + 47x

where y = total overhead costs in £ and x = machine hours:

(b) **Calculate the expected total overhead costs in 20Y2 if expected production activity is 3,100 machine hours and the expected cost index is 250.**

36 CFV

If a forecasting model based on total cost = fixed cost + variable costs is graphed, the equation is C = F + Vx and the intercept is £7,788.

If total costs are £14,520 and × is 3,300 then the gradient of the line, to two decimal places, is _____ .

PREPARING CASH BUDGETS

CASH RECEIPTS

37 An enterprise commenced business on 1 April 20X2. Revenue in April 20X2 was £20,000, and this is expected to increase at 2% a month. Cash sales represent the other 40% of revenue. Of the remaining sales the cash receipts are predicted to be 30% one month after sale, 65% two months after sale. The balance is potential irrecoverable debts, a provision is charged in the month of sale

(i) Calculate how much cash is expected to be received in June 20X2

(ii) Calculate the forecast closing receivables balance at the end of June 20X2

(iii) Calculate the irrecoverable debt provision for May 20X2

38 Jane limited sold 5,000 units of its only product in July 20X5 at a selling price of £60 each. Due to an increase in production costs, this price increases to £65 with effect from 1 August 20X5 and this is expected to reduce demand for August to 4,000 units. Thereafter, however, demand is expected to increase by 10% per month.

Cash sales account for 2,500 units per month and are expected to remain at this level. Credit sales account for the balance and receivables pay as follows:

(a) 60% by value in the month of sale, receiving a 2% discount

(b) 40% by value in the following month.

Credit sales in June were £103,500

What are the budgeted cash receipts in July, August and September 20X5?

39 Levison Entertainment has been trading for a number of years. Levison's owner, Ava, has called and asked for help in calculating her cash and credit sales. Actual sales values achieved are available for January and February and forecast sales values have been produced for March to June.

	Actual		Forecast			
	January	February	March	April	May	June
Total sales £	61,000	72,000	54,000	72,500	81,600	92,000

Levison Entertainment estimates that cash sales account for 8% of the total sales. The remaining 92% of sales are made on a credit basis. Levison Entertainment estimates that 30% of credit sales are received in the month after sale with the balance being received two months after sale.

(a) Calculate the timing of the credit sales receipts that would be included in a cash budget for Levison Entertainment for the period March to June.

	March	April	May	June
Monthly credit sales receipts £				

(b) The trade receivables balance at the end of June is forecast to be £ _____.

PRACTICE QUESTIONS : SECTION 1

40 Razor Bodyboards estimates that cash sales account for 15% of the total sales. The remaining 85% of sales are made on a credit basis.

	January	February	March
Total sales	51,000	62,000	44,000

Razor estimates that 60% of credit sales are received in the month after sale with 40% being received two months after sale.

(a) The receipts from both cash and credit sales to be shown in the cash budget for March will be?

A £48,960

B £50,120

C £55,560

D £58,260

(b) The trade receivables balance at the end of March is forecast to be £_____.

41 M Jones has been trading for a number of years. Sales volume has been forecast for January to May. Each picture sells for 20p.

Martin estimates that cash sales account for 40% of the total sales. The remaining sales are made on a credit basis.

Martin estimates that 60% of credit sales are received in the month after sale with the balance being received two months after sale.

	January	February	March	April	May
Sales volume (pictures)	1,500	2,000	1,800	1,900	2,100

Complete the table below to identify the total sales receipts forecast for April and May.

	April	May
Total sales receipts £		

Calculate the trade receivables balance at the end of May.

The trade receivables balance at the end of May is forecast to be £_____

42 Canvas Canopies has been trading for a number of years. The business has supplied information regarding its forecast sales, purchases and expenses.

Sales values have been forecast for January to May.

Canvas Canopies estimates that cash sales account for 15% of the total sales. The remaining 85% of sales are made on a credit basis.

	January	February	March	April	May
Total sales £	8,000	10,000	15,000	18,000	23,000

Canvas Canopies estimates that 70% of credit sales are received in the month after sale with the balance being received two months after sale.

KAPLAN PUBLISHING

AAT: CASH AND FINANCIAL MANAGEMENT

(a) **Complete the table below to calculate the total sales receipts forecast for April and May.**

	April £	May £
Total sales receipts		

(b) **Identify the forecast trade receivables balance at the end of May.**

The trade receivables balance at the end of May is forecast to be:

£_____

43 The sales information for the second 3 months of 20X2 for 'Light my Fire' is as follows:

- Sales to the retail trade are expected to be 120,000 candles in April, 125,000 in May and 130,000 in June. In addition we expect to sell 5,000 candles from our own shop in each of the next three months.
- Candles will be sold to the retail trade at £1.65. Sales made from our own shop will be made at £3 each.
- Sales from our own shop will be made for cash.
- Although it is our policy for all trade customers to pay within 30 days, for budgetary purposes you should assume that 30% of retail trade customers pay one month after the date of sale and 70% pay two months after the date of sale.
- The credit sales in February 20X2 were £145,000 and March 20X2 were £150,000.

Complete the table below to show the cash inflows for April to June 20X2

	April	May	June
Cash sales			
Credit sales receipts			
Total receipts			

44 Shirley Ltd has been trading for a number of years. Shirley's owner, Kelly, has called and asked for help in calculating their cash and credit sales.

The company receives cash for 50% of its sales. The balance of its revenue is received 30 days after sales.

Estimated sales figures and prices for the four months to 31st December 20Y1 are as follows:

		September	October	November	December
Sales units	000s	20	15	17	18
Selling price per unit	£	30	40	40	50

Calculate the cash inflows for October to December 20Y1.

	October	November	December
Cash sales			
Credit sales receipts			
Total cash received			

PRACTICE QUESTIONS : SECTION 1

45 Surfers Paradise Enterprises has been trading for a number of years.

Actual figures are available for April and May and forecast figures have been produced for June to September.

Cash sales account for 25% of the total sales. The remaining 75% of sales are made on a credit basis.

	Actual		Forecast			
	April	May	June	July	August	September
Total sales £	12,500	16,000	13,353	15,153	14,400	16,660

Surfers Paradise Enterprises estimates that 40% of credit sales are received in the month after sale, 20% two months after sale, with the balance being received three months after sale.

Calculate the credit sales receipts ready to include in a cash budget for Surfers Paradise Enterprises.

	July £	August £	September £
Credit sales receipts			

46 A company has the following budgeted sales figures:

Month 1   £90,000

Month 2   £105,000

Month 3   £120,000

Month 4   £108,000

80% of sales are on credit and the remainder are paid in cash. Credit customers paying in the month after sale are given a discount of 1.5%. Credit customers normally pay within the following time frame:

1 month after sale   40% of credit sales

2 months after sale   70% of credit sales

3 months after sale   98% of credit sales

There is an expectation that 2% of credit sales will become irrecoverable debts.

Calculate the total receipts expected in month 4.

AAT: CASH AND FINANCIAL MANAGEMENT

CASH PAYMENTS

47 A company has a budget, for two products A and B, as follows:

	Product A	Product B
Sales (units)	2,000	4,500
Production (units)	1,750	5,000
Labour:		
Skilled at £10/hour	2 hours/unit	2 hours/unit
Unskilled at £7/hour	3 hours/unit	4 hours/unit

Calculate the total labour cost to be included in the budget.

48 A job requires 2,400 standard labour hours for completion but it is anticipated that idle time will be 20% of the total time budgeted. If the wage rate is £10 per hour, what is the budgeted labour cost for the job, including the cost of the idle time?

A £19,200

B £24,000

C £28,800

D £30,000

49 M Singh pays her suppliers on the basis of 20% one month after date of purchase, 50% two months after purchase and the remainder three months after the date of purchase.

At the end March the balance on the trade payables is forecast to be:

	£
January	570
February	2,000
March	2,500
Trade payables at the end of March	5,070

Complete the table below to identify the value of trade payable at the end of March that will be paid in April and May.

	April £	May £
Settlement of trade payable		

50 Tarleton Ltd is preparing cash payment figures for a new division ready for inclusion in a cash budget. The following information is relevant to purchases of raw material.

	July £	August £	September £	October £	November £	December £
Opening inventory	4,000	8,400	9,100	9,000	11,600	12,600
Purchases	5,500	5,750	6,000	6,250	6,500	6,750
Closing inventory	(8,400)	(9,100)	(9,000)	(11,600)	(12,600)	(13,500)
Cost of sales	1,100	5,050	6,100	3,650	5,500	5,850

The company pays its supplier on the basis of 40% one month after the date of purchase and 60% two months after purchase.

(a) **At the end of September the balance of the trade payables is forecast to be:**

£ [   ]

(b) **Complete the table below to identify the value of trade payables that will be paid in October and November.**

	October £	November £
Purchases		

51 Canvas Canopies pays their suppliers on the basis of 40% one month after date of purchase, 20% two months after purchase and the remainder three months after the date of purchase.

At the end May the balance on the trade payables is forecast to be:

	£
January	5,280
February	8,640
March	16,800
Trade payables at the end of March	30,720

(a) **Complete the table below to identify the value of trade payables at the end of March that will be paid in April and May.**

	April £	May £
Settlement of trade payables		

A new machine is to be purchased in January at a total cost of £60,000. Payment for the machine is to be made in three equal monthly instalments, beginning in January.

The machine is to be depreciated monthly on a straight-line basis at 20% per annum. This has been included in the expenses of the business.

Expenses are paid in the month they are incurred.

(b) **Complete the table below to show the expenses to be included in the cash budget.**

	January £	February £	March £	April £	May £
Expenses	4,512	4,951	5,541	5,745	6,785
Total cost to be included in cash budget					

52 North Ltd is preparing cash payment figures ready for inclusion in a cash budget.

	October £000	November £000	December £000
Trade payables	120	120	120
Direct labour	210	210	560
Administration cost	60	60	60
Production costs	105	105	280
Distribution costs	21	21	56
Non-current asset purchase	300	25	0
Total payments	**816**	**541**	**1,076**

Workings:

- Production each month = following month's sales:
  - October production = 15,000 units (Nov sales)
  - November production = 15,000 units (Dec sales)
  - December production = 40,000 units (Jan sales)

- Trade payables (paid 30 days after purchase, materials £8/unit):
  - October pays September purchases: 15,000 × £8 = £120,000
  - November pays October purchases: 15,000 × £8 = £120,000
  - December pays November purchases: 15,000 × £8 = £120,000

- Direct labour (2 hrs × £7 = £14/unit):
  - Oct: 15,000 × £14 = £210,000
  - Nov: 15,000 × £14 = £210,000
  - Dec: 40,000 × £14 = £560,000

- Administration cost: £90,000 − £30,000 depreciation = £60,000 per month

- Production costs (£10 − £3 depreciation = £7 cash per unit):
  - Oct: 15,000 × £7 = £105,000
  - Nov: 15,000 × £7 = £105,000
  - Dec: 40,000 × £7 = £280,000

- Distribution costs (10% of direct labour):
  - Oct: £21,000; Nov: £21,000; Dec: £56,000

- Non-current asset purchase: £300,000 Sept, £300,000 Oct, £25,000 Nov

PRACTICE QUESTIONS : SECTION 1

53 South Ltd is preparing cash payment figures for inclusion in a cash budget. The following information is relevant to the payment patterns for purchases, wages and expenses.

- Purchases are calculated as 42% of the next month's forecast sales and are paid two months after the date of purchase.

	Actual			Forecast		
	Jan £	Feb £	Mar £	Apr £	May £	June £
Total sales	100,000	120,000	118,000	124,000	130,000	136,000

- Wages are paid in the month that they are incurred and expenses are paid the month after they are incurred. The actual and forecast figures for wages and expenses are:

	Actual			Forecast		
	Jan £	Feb £	Mar £	Apr £	May £	June £
Wages	7,000	7,200	7,250	7,800	8,100	8,500
Expenses	11,000	11,100	12,000	12,200	12,400	12,900

- A new machine is to be purchased in February at a total cost of £39,000. Payment for the machine is to be made in three equal monthly instalments, beginning in March.

What is the total cash out flow in May?

A £82,860

B £85,380

C £85,580

D £87,900

54 Bailey Rae Ltd produces garden gnomes.

Labour costs include hourly paid employees and four-weekly paid employees. The labour costs for hourly paid employees are calculated based on the number of hours worked multiplied by a standard hourly rate of £12. Hourly paid employees are paid overtime at a premium of 25%. The company also employs a supervisor who receives an annual salary of £23,400. The year is divided into 13 four week periods.

Any overtime payments are paid in the following period, once the overtime has been signed off.

	February £	March £	April £	May £
Forecast standard hours	2,000	1,800	1,950	1,850
Forecast overtime hours	200	150	170	120

Calculate the total payments for labour in April and May.

	April	May
Total labour costs		

AAT: CASH AND FINANCIAL MANAGEMENT

55 Jump Ltd purchases raw materials from Bounce Ltd for £15 per unit. Purchases were 19,000 units for period 7 and 20,500 units for period 8. Forecast purchases for the rest of the year are as follows:

Units	Period 9	Period 10	Period 11	Period 12
Purchases	20,000	21,000	20,500	22,000

Jump Ltd currently pays Bounce Ltd as follows:

- Period of purchase 10%
- Period following period of purchase 50%
- Balance to be paid two periods following the period of purchase

A competitor to Bounce Ltd has started offering the same raw materials at a price of £10 per unit and would be able to start supplying to Jump Ltd in Period 9. However their payment terms are:

- Period of purchase 60%
- Period following the period of purchase 40%

Bounce Ltd has realised that their competitor is undercutting their prices, and is now offering Jump Ltd the following settlement discounts and payment terms for period 9 and onwards

Option 1 12% discount for making full payment in the period of purchase

Option 2 6% discount on the whole purchase, for making a payment of 50% in the period of purchase and the remaining 50% in the period following the period of purchase

Calculate the forecast cash payments in periods 10, 11 and 12 under the current purchase and payments terms, if Jump Ltd changed supplier and for each of the two discount options from Bounce Ltd.

	Period 10 £	Period 11 £	Period 12 £
Current terms			
Competitor terms			
Option 1			
Option 2			

56 D plc operates a retail business. Purchases are sold at cost plus 25%. The management team is preparing the cash budget and has gathered the following data:

1. The budgeted sales are as follows:

Month	£000
July	100
August	90
September	125
October	140

2. It is management policy to hold inventory at the end of each month which is sufficient to meet sales demand in the next half month. Sales are budgeted to occur evenly during each month.

3. Payables are paid one month after the purchase has been made.

PRACTICE QUESTIONS : SECTION 1

Calculate the entries for 'cash paid to suppliers for purchases' that will be shown in the cash budget for:

(i) August

(ii) September

(iii) October

57 A business pays its suppliers on the basis of 20% one month after the date of purchase, 50% two months after the date of purchase and 30% three months after the date of purchase.

At the end of June the balance of trade payables is forecast to be:

	£
Balance from April	6,000
Balance from May	19,200
Balance from June	28,400
Trade payables at the end of June	53,600

Complete the table to identify the value of trade payables at the end of June that will be collected in July and August

	July £	August £
Settlement of trade payables		

58 The direct labour costs for a business include both standard working hours and overtime. These costs are split between 80% standard working hours and 20% overtime.

Standard working hours are paid in the month worked whilst overtime is paid in the following month. In addition to this; a performance bonus is paid quarterly; the next payment will be in September and will be £125,000. The overtime for June was £90,000.

In addition to the direct labour costs, employer's National Insurance payments are 10% for standard working hours and 12% for overtime and the performance bonus. This is paid in the month following payment of the appropriate element of the direct labour cost. The outstanding payment for the June employer's National Insurance is £32,000.

The direct labour costs are as follows:

July   £340,000

August   £360,000

September   £350,000

October   £400,000

(a) **Calculate the total payments made in July, August, September and October for direct labour costs, performance bonus and employer's National Insurance contributions.**

Month	July	August	September	October
Total payment				

(b) **What are the employer's National Insurance contributions on the overtime paid in November?**

AAT: CASH AND FINANCIAL MANAGEMENT

CASH BUDGETS

59 The following data are available for GHK Ltd for June, July and August:

	June £	July £	August £
Sales	45,000	50,000	60,000
Wages	12,000	13,000	14,500
Overheads	8,500	9,500	9,000

The following information is available regarding direct materials:

	June £	July £	August £	September £
Opening inventory	5,000	3,500	6,000	4,000
Material usage	8,000	9,000	10,000	
Closing inventory	3,500	6,000	4,000	

Notes:

1 10% of sales are for cash, the balance is received the following month. The amount to be received in June for May's sales is £29,500.

2 Wages are paid in the month they are incurred.

3 Overheads include £1,500 per month for depreciation. Overheads are settled the month following. £6,500 is to be paid in June for May's overheads.

4 Direct materials are paid for in the month purchased.

5 The opening cash balance in June is £11,750.

6 A tax bill of £25,000 is to be paid in July.

Required:

(a) **Calculate the amount of direct material purchases in EACH of the months of June, July and August.**

(b) **Prepare cash budgets for June, July and August.**

(c) **Describe briefly the benefits of preparing cash budgets.**

60 Campbell Ltd buys goods in bulk from a French manufacturing company, packs them and then sells them on to retailers.

- Sales for May and June 20X6 were £10,000 each month and are forecast to increase by 10% each month from July 20X6 onwards.

- There are no cash sales and receivables are expected to settle as follows:

    (i)   25% in the month of sale

    (ii) 60% in the month following sale

    (iii) 15% in month two months after sale.

- Loose product (unpacked) is bought in the month in which it is sold. Purchases for May and June were €7,080 each month, and are forecast to increase by 9% each month from July onwards. Suppliers allow one month's credit. The exchange rate is €1:£0.7203

KAPLAN PUBLISHING

PRACTICE QUESTIONS : SECTION 1

- Packaging costs amount to £1,800 per month paid in the month incurred.
- Sundry expenses amount to £800 per month.
- Depreciation is £1,000 per month.
- At 30 June 20X6, the bank balance was £6,000 overdrawn.

Prepare a cash flow forecast for the 3 months ended 30 September 20X6 (round your values to the nearest whole pound).

61 The cash budget for SDS Ltd for the three months ended August has been partially completed. The following information is to be incorporated and the cash budget completed.

- A bank loan of £30,000 has been negotiated and this will be paid into the business bank account in July.
- The loan term is 10 months beginning in August. Interest of 8% is added at the beginning of the loan term and monthly repayments include both capital and interest elements.
- New fixtures and fittings are to be purchased in July at a cost of £10,000. The cost is to be spread over 5 monthly instalments starting in August.
- If SDS uses its bank overdraft facility, interest is payable monthly and is estimated at 2% of the previous months overdraft balance. The interest is to be rounded to the nearest £.
- At 1 June the balance of the bank overdraft was £5,000.

Using the information above, complete the cash budget for SDS for the three months ending August.

Cash inflows should be entered as positive figures and cash outflows as negative figures. Zeros must be entered where appropriate to achieve full marks.

	June £	July £	August £
RECEIPTS			
Cash sales	1,100	1,200	2,300
Credit sales	40,810	60,540	70,990
Bank loan			
Total receipts			
PAYMENTS			
Purchases	−42,111	−20,804	−41,305
Wages	−18,000	−11,000	−12,100
Expenses	−2,555	−1,543	−1,100
Capital expenditure			
Bank loan repayment			
Overdraft interest			
Total payments			
Net cash flow			
Opening bank balance			
Closing bank balance			

KAPLAN PUBLISHING

62 The cash budget for Bank Industries for the three months ended 30th June needs to be completed using the following information.

- Actual and forecast sales are as follows:

	Actual		Forecast		
	February	March	April	May	June
Total sales £	32,500	34,800	40,500	42,000	45,750

- 20% of cash is received in the month of sale, 30% one month after sale and the remainder two months after sale.

- Credit purchases were £15,000 in February and are forecast to increase by 4% each month. Payments are made one month after purchase.

- Wages are forecast to be £8,000 each month.

- Other expenses, paid one month in arrears, are as follows:

	Actual		Forecast		
	February	March	April	May	June
Expenses £	5,000	4,750	4,950	5,125	5,050

- A bank loan of £100,000 has been negotiated and this will be paid into the business bank account in April. The loan term is 20 months beginning in May. Interest is to be paid at £50 per month for the first year, starting in May.

- When Bank Industries uses its bank overdraft facility, interest is payable monthly and is estimated at 2% of the previous month's overdraft balance. The interest is to be rounded to the nearest £.

- Bank Industries has to pay tax of £60,000 in April.

- At 1 April the balance of the bank account was £50,000 in credit.

Using the information above, complete the cash budget for Bank Industries for the three months ending June.

Cash inflows should be entered as positive figures and cash outflows as negative figures. Zeros must be entered where appropriate to achieve full marks. Round your answers to the nearest whole £.

	April £	May £	June £
RECEIPTS			
Cash sales			
Credit sales			
Bank loan			
Total receipts			
PAYMENTS			
Purchases			
Wages			
Expenses			
Tax payment			
Bank loan repayment			
Overdraft interest			
Total payments			
Net cash flow			
Opening bank balance			
Closing bank balance			

63 The cash budget for Surfers Paradise Enterprises for the three months ended 30 September needs to be completed.

- Actual and forecast sales are as follows:

	Actual		Forecast		
	May	June	July	August	September
Total sales £	9,000	10,500	11,000	13,000	16,000

- 15% of cash is received in the month of sale, 45% one month after sale and the remainder two months after sale.

- Credit purchases were £7,000 in June and are forecast to increase by 3% each month. Payments are made one month after purchase.

- Wages are forecast to be £4,000 each month.

- Other expenses, paid one month after being incurred, are as follows:

	Actual		Forecast		
	May	June	July	August	September
Expenses £	1,500	1,250	1,750	2,000	1,800

- A bank loan of £12,960 has been negotiated and this will be paid into the business bank account in July. The loan attracts 10% interest calculated on the amount of the loan advanced in July. The interest is added at the beginning of the loan term. The capital and interest elements of the bank loan are to be repaid in 36 equal monthly instalments beginning in August.

AAT: CASH AND FINANCIAL MANAGEMENT

- Surfers Paradise Enterprises receives 0.5% interest based on a credit closing balance, received one month in arrears. The interest is to be rounded to the nearest £.

- Overdraft interest is payable monthly and is estimated at 1% of the previous month's overdraft balance. The interest is to be rounded to the nearest £.

- Surfers Paradise Enterprises will be making a dividend payment to shareholders of £15,000 in July.

- At 1 July the balance of the bank account was £3,600 in credit.

Using the information above, complete the cash budget for Surfers Paradise Enterprises for the three months ending 30th September.

Cash inflows should be entered as positive figures and cash outflows as negative figures. Zeros must be entered where appropriate to achieve full marks. Round your answers to the nearest whole £.

	July £	August £	September £
RECEIPTS			
Cash sales			
Credit sales			
Bank loan			
Interest receivable			
Total receipts			
PAYMENTS			
Purchases			
Wages			
Expenses			
Dividend payment			
Bank loan repayment			
Overdraft interest			
Total payments			
Net cash flow			
Opening bank balance			
Closing bank balance			

64 Jump Ltd has provided the following partially completed cash budget for month 3 and month 4. Further information has been provided to determine the cash inflows and outflows from the company.

- The company rents out part of its property with effect from month 4. The rent is £31,200 per annum and is payable in equal monthly instalments on the first day of each month.

- The company has got £500,000 invested in a fixed rate account, paying interest of 5% per annum. The company has chosen to have this interest paid monthly.

- The company received payment for the sale of a non-current asset in month 3. The profit from the sale was £7,000 and the asset originally cost £48,000 and has been depreciated by 50%. (Ignore VAT)

PRACTICE QUESTIONS : SECTION 1

- The company bought a non-current asset in month 2. The new asset cost £54,000 and paid 45% in month 2. The remaining balance is to be paid in six equal instalments commencing in month 3. (Ignore VAT).

- The company has a mortgage on their premises. The purchase cost of the premises was £750,000 and the mortgage is 80% LTV. The mortgage is for 15 years and interest is charged on the initial balance at 4.5% per annum. Payments are made monthly.

- Jump Ltd prepares its VAT return for the previous quarter ending month 12. The sales for the quarter were £510,100 net with purchases of £340,100. The VAT rate is 20%. Any VAT payment or refund with be made or received in month 3.

- The bank balance for Month 3 was £160,000

Using the information provided, complete the cash balance for the company for Month 3 and 4.

Note

- Cash inflows should be entered as positive figures
- Cash outflows should be entered as negative figures (use brackets or minus sign)
- Round to the nearest whole pound throughout
- If a cell does not require an entry, leave it blank

	Month 3 £	Month 4 £
RECEIPTS		
Sales receipts	672,450	682,670
Rental income		
Investment income		
Sale of non-current asset		
Total receipts		
PAYMENTS		
Purchases	−40,150	−50,200
Wages and salaries	−94,700	−92,100
General Expenses	−6,000	−5,000
Mortgage payment		
VAT payment to HMRC		
Purchase of non-current assets		
Overdraft interest		
Total payments		
Net cash flow		
Opening bank balance		
Closing bank balance		

65 The cash budget for Gibbon Ltd has been partially completed for two periods. The following information is to be incorporated and the cash budget completed.

- In an earlier period Gibbon Ltd made an insurance claim of £125,000. The insurer rejected 10% of this claim and will make a payment to Gibbon Ltd of 80% of the accepted liability in period 4, the remainder will be made in period 6

- The US subsidiary is due to pay a dividend of USD 50,000 in period 5. The exchange rate to be used to convert the receipt into GBP is USD 1.22:GBP 1

- A statue was purchased in period 3. It cost £10,000 and will be sold with a margin of 20% in period 5.

- Following the retirement of the CEO, a recruitment company was employed to search for a replacement. This person has been found and appointed. The fees and commission amount to a flat rate of £7,000 plus 20% of the starting salary of £150,000, payable in Period 5.

- Payroll cost for period 4 to 6 are in the table below. 12% of the payroll represents normal deductions from employees which are paid to HMRC in the month following the month that the cost is incurred. The employees receive their pay on the last Thursday of the month in which their pay is earned. The employer's NIC is paid to HMRC at the same time the employees' deductions are paid.

Forecast data	Period 4	Period 5	Period 6
Payroll	80,000	80,300	80,500
Employer's NIC	16,000	16,060	16,100

Using the information, complete the cash budget for the company for periods 5 and 6

Note:

- Cash inflows should be entered as positive figures
- Cash outflows should be entered as negative figures (use brackets)
- Round to the nearest whole pound throughout
- If a cell does not require an entry, leave it blank

Cash budget	Period 5 £	Period 6 £
Receipts		
Receipts from sales	100,500	106,250
Insurance claim		
Dividend receipt		
Receipt from sale of statue		
Total receipts		
Payments		
Purchases	(8,510)	(9,400)
Payroll payments to employees		
Payments to HMRC		
Recruitment cost of the CEO		
Other expenses	(12,050)	(16,507)
Total payments		
Net cash flow		
Opening bank balance	8,250	
Closing bank balance		

ANALYSING AND MONITORING CASH BUDGETS

SENSITIVITY ANALYSIS

66 Complete the following sentences by selecting the correct options:

Offering prompt payment discounts to customers should **[increase/decrease]** the time taken to recover debts. However, it will also **[increase/reduce]** the total cash received.

This should **[increase/decrease]** liquidity but **[increase/reduce]** the overall profitability.

67 Complete the following sentence by selecting the correct options:

Taking advantage of early settlement discounts offered by suppliers will **[increase/reduce]** the amount we pay overall but having to pay **[earlier/later]** may mean there is a **[bigger/smaller]** strain on our cash flows.

68 A cash budget has been prepared for Worsley Ltd for the next five periods.

The budget was prepared based on the following sales volumes and a selling price of £50 per item.

	Period 1	Period 2	Period 3	Period 4	Period 5
Sales volume (items)	1,800	1,900	2,050	1,890	2,150

The pattern of cash receipts used in the budget assumed 30% of sales were received in the month of sale and the remaining 70% in the month following sale.

AAT: CASH AND FINANCIAL MANAGEMENT

In the light of current economic trends, Worsley Ltd needs to adjust its cash budget to take account of the following:

- The selling price from period 1 will be reduced by 20% per item.
- The pattern of sales receipts changes to 10% of sales received in the month of sale, 50% in the month following sale and the remaining 40% two months after sale.

(a) Use the table below to calculate the effect of the changes in the forecast amounts and timing of cash receipts for periods 3, 4 and 5:

	Period 1 £	Period 2 £	Period 3 £	Period 4 £	Period 5 £
Original value of forecast sales					
Original timing of receipts					
Revised value of forecast sales					
Revised timing of receipts					

The company has managed to negotiate extended payment terms with its suppliers. The original budget was prepared on the basis of paying suppliers in the month following purchase. The revised payment terms allow for settlement of 20% in the month following purchase with the remaining payment two months after purchase.

The original budgeted purchases figures were:

	Period 1 £	Period 2 £	Period 3 £	Period 4 £	Period 5 £
Purchases	21,200	22,354	28,601	21,660	29,500

(b) Use the table below to calculate the effect of the changes in the timing of purchase payments for periods 3, 4 and 5:

	Period 3 £	Period 4 £	Period 5 £
Original timing of payments			
Revised timing of payments			

Worsley Ltd has always tried to operate without utilising a bank overdraft and the original cash budget identified that an overdraft would not be required for periods 3, 4 or 5.

(c) Using your calculations from parts (a) and (b), complete the table to show the effect of the changes to sales receipts and purchase payments on the budgeted bank balance for periods 3, 4 and 5.

	Period 3 £	Period 4 £	Period 5 £
Original net cash flow	5,632	5,162	5,893
Changes in sales receipts			
Changes in purchase payments			
Revised net cash flow			
Opening bank balance	8,597		
Closing bank balance			

69 A cash budget has been prepared for Jones Ltd for the next five periods.

The budget was prepared based on the following sales volumes and a selling price of £150 per item.

	Period 1	Period 2	Period 3	Period 4	Period 5
Sales volume (items)	800	900	650	890	750

The pattern of cash receipts used in the budget assumed 20% of sales were received in the month of sale and the remaining 80% in the month following sale.

In the light of current economic trends, Jones Ltd needs to adjust its cash budget to take account of the following:

- The sales volume for each period will be reduced by 30%.

- The pattern of sales receipts changes to 20% of sales received in the month of sale, 60% in the month following sale and the remaining 20% two months after sale.

(a) Use the table below to calculate the effect of the changes in the forecast amounts and timing of cash receipts for periods 3, 4 and 5:

	Period 1 £	Period 2 £	Period 3 £	Period 4 £	Period 5 £
Original value of forecast sales					
Original timing of receipts					
Revised value of forecast sales					
Revised timing of receipts					

Purchases are based on the budgeted sales volume for the next month. Each item is purchased for £90. Jones Ltd has managed to negotiate extended payment terms with its suppliers. The original budget was prepared on the basis of paying suppliers in the month following purchase. The revised payment terms allow for settlement of 60% in the month following purchase with the remaining payment two months after purchase.

(b) Use the table below to calculate the effect of the changes in the timing of purchase payments for periods 3, 4 and 5:

	Period 3 £	Period 4 £	Period 5 £
Original timing of payments			
Revised timing of payments			

Jones Ltd has always tried to operate without utilising a bank overdraft and the original cash budget identified that an overdraft would not be required for periods 3, 4 or 5.

(c) Using your calculations from parts (a) and (b), complete the table to show the effect of the changes to sales receipts and purchase payments on the budgeted bank balance for periods 3, 4 and 5.

	Period 3 £	Period 4 £	Period 5 £
Original net cash flow	52,362	51,986	53,695
Changes in sales receipts			
Changes in purchase payments			
Revised net cash flow			
Opening bank balance	18,597		
Closing bank balance			

70 A cash budget has been prepared for a new division of TanTan Ltd for the next five periods.

The budget was prepared based on the following sales volumes and a selling price of £95 per item.

	Period 1	Period 2	Period 3	Period 4	Period 5
Forecast sales £	95,000	104,500	99,750	152,000	166,250

The pattern of cash receipts used in the budget assumed 30% of sales were received in the month of sale and the remaining 70% in the month following sale.

	Period 1	Period 2	Period 3	Period 4	Period 5
Original forecast sales receipts £	28,500	97,850	103,075	115,425	156,275

TanTan Ltd wishes to encourage payment of debts so it is going to introduce a settlement discount for early repayment. The pattern of sales receipts is planned to be:

- 60% of sales received in the month of sale with a discount of 2%
- 30% in the month following sale
- 10% two months after sale.

(a) Complete the table below to calculate the sales receipts expected in periods 1–5:

	Period 1 £	Period 2 £	Period 3 £	Period 4 £	Period 5 £
Period 1 sales					
Period 2 sales					
Period 3 sales					
Period 4 sales					
Period 5 sales					
Revised forecast sales receipts					

(b) Complete the sentence below:

Total receipts from sales in periods 1 to 3 **increase/decrease** by _____% if the settlement discount is offered.

71

A cash budget has been prepared for Higson Ltd for the next five periods.

The budget was prepared based on the following sales volumes and a selling price of £18 per item.

	Period 1	Period 2	Period 3	Period 4	Period 5
Sales volume (items)	1,800	1,900	2,050	1,890	2,150

The pattern of cash receipts used in the budget assumed 35% of sales were received in the month of sale, 25% in the month following sale and 40% two months after sale.

Higson Ltd has heard that one of its customers is going out of business and will not be ordering any more goods from them. This customer had planned to buy 500 units in period 1 and 250 units in period 3. The budget needs to be adjusted to take account of this.

(a) Use the table below to calculate the effect of the changes in the forecast amounts of the cash receipts for periods 3, 4 and 5:

	Period 1 £	Period 2 £	Period 3 £	Period 4 £	Period 5 £
Original value of forecast sales	32,400	34,200	36,900	34,020	38,700
Revised value of forecast sales	23,400	34,200	32,400	34,020	38,700
Original timing of receipts			34,425	34,812	36,810
Revised timing of receipts			29,250	33,687	35,010

Purchases are based on the budgeted sales volume for the next month. The company will be able to adjust the purchases based on the changes in sales. Each item costs £10 to buy. The budget was prepared on the basis of paying suppliers 35% in the month following purchase with the remaining payment two months after purchase.

(b) Use the table below to calculate the effect on the cash flow of the changes in the volume of purchases for periods 3, 4 and 5:

	Period 3 £	Period 4 £	Period 5 £
Payment for purchases	18,650	18,315	19,810

Higson Ltd has always tried to operate without utilising a bank overdraft, and the original cash budget identified that an overdraft would not be required for periods 3, 4 or 5.

(c) Calculate from the budgeted bank balance at the end of period 5.

	£
Opening bank balance period 3	3,200
Total sales receipts	97,947
Total purchase payments	56,775
Closing bank balance period 5	44,372

AAT: CASH AND FINANCIAL MANAGEMENT

72 A cash budget has been prepared for Barossa Ltd for the next five periods.

The budget was prepared based a selling price of £14 per item.

	Period 1	Period 2	Period 3	Period 4	Period 5
Sales value £	30,100	30,800	32,620	31,640	33,600

The pattern of cash receipts used in the budget assumed 50% of sales were received in the month of sale and the remaining 50% in the month following sale.

In the light of current economic trends, Barossa Ltd needs to adjust its cash budget to take account of the following:

- The selling price from period 1 will be reduced by 5% per item.
- The sales volume will also be reduced by 8% (round to the nearest whole item).
- The pattern of sales receipts changes to 15% of sales received in the month of sale, 40% in the month following sale and the remaining 45% two months after sale.

(a) Use the table below to calculate the revised forecast sales and revised timing of cash receipts for periods 3, 4 and 5:

	Period 1 £	Period 2 £	Period 3 £	Period 4 £	Period 5 £
Revised value of forecast sales					
Revised timing of receipts					

The company has managed to negotiate new payment terms with its suppliers. The original budget was prepared on the basis of paying suppliers in the month following purchase. The revised payment terms allow for settlement of 40% in the month of purchase with a 3% settlement discount, 30% in the month following purchase with the remaining payment two months after purchase.

The original budgeted purchase figures were:

	Period 1 £	Period 2 £	Period 3 £	Period 4 £	Period 5 £
Purchases	8,580	7,600	6,820	10,740	11,310

(b) Use the table below to calculate the revised timing of purchase payments for periods 3, 4 and 5:

	Period 3 £	Period 4 £	Period 5 £
Revised timing of payments			

Barossa Ltd has always tried to operate without utilising a bank overdraft and the original cash budget identified that an overdraft would not be required for periods 3, 4 or 5.

(c) Using your calculations from parts (a) and (b) plus the information regarding the original receipts and payments, complete the table to show the effect of the changes to sales receipts and purchase payments on the budgeted bank balance for periods 3, 4 and 5.

	Period 3 £	Period 4 £	Period 5 £
Original net cash flow	276	153	219
Changes in sales receipts			
Changes in purchase payments			
Revised net cash flow			
Opening bank balance	790		
Closing bank balance			

73 The draft cash budget of Splish Inc shows the following:

	Period 1 £	Period 2 £	Period 3 £
Receipts	70,000	75,000	78,000
Payments			
Purchases	15,000	17,500	18,900
Other production expenses	6,000	6,200	6,700
Wages and salaries	8,250	8,800	9,000
Rent	12,000	12,000	12,000
Total Payments	41,250	44,400	46,500

Additional information has now been received:

- A trade discount of 4% has been negotiated on purchases, with no change in payment pattern
- Other production expenses will increase by 7%, with no change in payment pattern
- Wages and salaries are paid in the month they are incurred, and a pay rise of 2.5% has been agreed which will come into effect in period 2
- Rent is paid one month in advance and rent will increase by £400 in period 3.

(a) **Prepare a revised payments schedule to take account of the changes outlined above. Do not use minus figures.**

	Period 1 £	Period 2 £	Period 3 £
Payments			
Purchases			
Other production expenses			
Wages and salaries			
Rent			
Total payments			

(b) The effect of the changes to payments is to **increase/decrease** the quarterly cash outflows by £_____ .

AAT: CASH AND FINANCIAL MANAGEMENT

74 The draft cash receipts and payments budget for a company for the quarter to March has been prepared as follows:

	January £	February £	March £	Total £
Sales receipts	30,000	24,000	35,000	89,000
Payments				
Material	7,500	6,000	8,750	22,250
Labour	9,000	7,200	10,500	26,700
Overheads	7,500	6,600	8,250	22,350

- When the budget was set the selling price was £20. It has been decided to increase the selling price by 10% but this will reduce volume by 12%. All sales are made on a cash basis.

- Material cost is £5 per unit made. Materials are paid for in the month of purchase and no inventory of material is maintained.

- Each unit is forecast to take 0.5 hours to make. Labour is paid at £12 per hour. Due to the learning effect it is now taking employees 0.25 hours to make a unit and, to reward this new efficiency, wages have been increased to £14 per hour.

- Overheads include a fixed cost of £3,000 and a variable cost of £3 per unit.

(a) Prepare revised figures for the cash budget for January to March.

	January £	February £	March £	Total £
Sales receipts				
Payments				
Material				
Labour				
Overheads				

The opening cash balance for January was £14,750.

(b) Calculate the original cash balance at the end of March and then calculate the revised cash balance once the budgeted amendments have been applied. Use minus signs to indicate a negative impact on the cash balance.

	£
Original closing cash balance at 31 March	
Change in sales receipts	
Change in material cost	
Change in labour cost	
Change in overhead cost	
Revised closing cash balance at 31 March	

Calculate the effect the above will have on the cash flow of the company for periods 1 to 3.

The cumulative cash flow for period 1 to 3 will **increase/decrease** by £ ☐

75 Yanu plc is planning on replacing some of its machinery. It will cost £1.5 million and will be paid in equal amounts in periods 1 and 2. The new machines will increase productivity by 10,000 units a period; all these units will be sold in the month of production at £50 each. The cash will be received 50% in the month of sale and 50% the month following sale.

Calculate the effect the above will have on the cash flow of the company for periods 1 to 3.

The cumulative cash flow for period 1 to 3 will **increase/decrease** by £ 250,000

76 Kovich Ltd thinks that they will need to pay overtime due to increased production for the next 4 weeks. The overtime premium is 50% of the normal hourly wage. The total overtime payment is £10.50. It is thought that the hours will increase by 25%, currently there are 50 employees, working a 37 hour week. The extra production will lead to an increase in units available to sell. The increase in sales will amount to an extra £25,000 in cash receipts.

Calculate the effect the above will have on the cash flow of Kovich Ltd over the next 4 weeks.

The cumulative cash flow for the next four weeks will **increase/decrease** by £ 5,575

77 Gibbons Ltd has an agreement to pay its major supplier for purchases as follows:

30% in month of purchases

25% in the month following purchase

45% two months following month of purchase

The value of the materials expected to be purchased in January, February, March and April is as follows:

January £230,000

February £290,000

March £230,000

April £270,000

The supplier has announced that a discount of 2% will be offered on all purchases over £250,000 if payment is received in the month of sale. To take advantage of this Gibbon Ltd has decided to equally divide its expected purchases over the next four months but will pay as follows:

50% in the month of purchase

10% in the month following the month of purchase

40% two months following month of purchase

As January is the start of the new reporting period, Gibbon Ltd has decided to pay all outstanding trade payables at the end of December.

(a) Calculate the forecast purchase payments in January, February, March and April, taking advantage of the discount on the revised payment terms. VAT can be ignored.

Month	January £	February £	March £	April £
Forecast purchase payments				

(b) Calculate the total savings made over the four months on the revised payment terms.

MONITORING CASH BUDGETS

78 The quarterly budget and actual figures for Heavier Goth Ltd are provided below:

	Budget £	Actual £
Receipts from receivables	65,664	58,844
Cash sales	2,890	3,844
Payments to payables	(46,666)	(35,100)
Cash purchases	(1,000)	(1,200)
Capital expenditure	–	(24,500)
Wages and salaries	(7,690)	(5,600)
General expenses	(17,500)	(16,000)
Net cash flow	(4,302)	(19,712)
Opening bank balance	7,500	7,500
Closing bank balance	3,198	(12,212)

(a) Prepare a reconciliation of budgeted cash flow with actual cash flow for the quarter. Select the appropriate description for each entry.

	Variance £	Adverse/Favourable
Budgeted closing bank balance		
Receipts from receivables		
Cash sales		
Payments to payables		
Cash purchases		
Capital expenditure		
Wages and salaries		
General expenses		
Actual closing bank balance		

(b) What action could the organisation have taken to avoid an overdrawn bank balance (select one option)?

    A   Chased customers to pay sooner and delayed payments to payables

    B   Increased cash sales through better marketing

    C   Delayed capital expenditure

    D   Negotiated lower wages payments to employees

(c) Match each cause of a variance listed on the left with a possible course of action on the right.

Cause	Course of action
Rates of income tax have increased labour costs	Improve credit control
Customers are buying lower value products	Change suppliers
Suppliers are insisting on earlier payments	Reduce hours worked
Customers are taking more days to settle their debts	Negotiate early settlement discount
Prices of raw materials have increased	Actively market more expensive product lines

79 The budget and actual figures for GFD Ltd are provided below, along with the variances.

	Budget £	Actual £	Variance £
Receipts from receivables	9,664	8,844	820 A
Cash sales	890	844	46 A
Payments to payables	(3,666)	(5,100)	1,434 A
Cash purchases	(100)	(1,200)	1,100 A
Capital expenditure	–	(14,500)	14,500 A
Wages and salaries	(690)	(600)	90 F
Net cash flow	6,098	(11,712)	
Opening bank balance	500	500	
Closing bank balance	6,598	(11,212)	

(a) Provide possible reasons why the variances might have occurred.

(b) Suggest corrective actions and identify implications for future budget setting, where appropriate.

80 Complete the table below by calculating the missing figures.

Use minus signs (not brackets) where appropriate and put A into the table to denote an adverse difference and F to denote a favourable difference.

	Budgeted £	Actual £	Variance £	A/F
RECEIPTS				
Cash sales	4,200	3,800		
Credit sales		48,000	5,900	F
Total receipts				
PAYMENTS				
Cash purchases	−500		700	A
Credit purchases		−35,100	7,100	A
Labour costs	−2,500	−3,200		
Capital expenditure	−8,000	−6,000		
General expenses	−4,000		200	F
Total payments				
Net cash flow				

81 The quarterly budget and actual figures for an organisation are provided below:

	Budget £	Actual £
Receipts from receivables	56,423	51,667
Cash sales	7,350	6,780
Payments to payables	(42,618)	(44,791)
Cash purchases	(5,600)	(6,540)
Capital expenditure	–	(12,000)
Wages and salaries	(6,200)	(2,600)
General expenses	(6,600)	(2,464)
Net cash flow	2,755	(9,948)
Opening bank balance	3,700	3,700
Closing bank balance	6,455	(6,248)

(a) Prepare a reconciliation of budgeted cash flow with actual cash flow for the quarter.

	£	Adverse or favourable
Budgeted closing bank balance		
Receipts from receivables		
Cash sales		
Payments to payables		
Cash purchases		
Capital expenditure		
Wages and salaries		
General expenses		
Actual closing bank balance		

(b) Explain what actions the organisation should have taken to avoid an overdrawn bank balance?

82 The budget and actual figures for SPR Ltd are provided below. A variance which is 5% or more of the original budget is deemed to be significant and needs to be investigated.

	Budgeted £	Actual £
RECEIPTS		
Credit sales	95,651	89,891
Investment income	15,360	12,569
Total receipts	111,011	102,460
PAYMENTS		
Cash purchases	8,354	8,369
Credit purchases	47,532	48,985
Labour costs	2,200	2,000
Capital expenditure	25,000	32,000
General expenses	5,951	5,713
Total payments	89,037	97,067
Net cash flow	21,974	5,393

Further information has been made available:

- A machine in the production department broke down and had to be replaced.
- There has been a recent reduction in the bank base rate from 1.5% to 0.5%

Identify each of the significant variances for the period. Provide possible reasons why the variance might have occurred, suggest corrective actions where appropriate, and identify implications for future budget setting.

AAT: CASH AND FINANCIAL MANAGEMENT

LIQUIDITY MANAGEMENT

LIQUIDITY AND WORKING CAPITAL

83 Which one of the following is the main function of liquidity management?

    A   keeping cash in the bank

    B   making a profit

    C   meeting any liabilities due

    D   investing in capital expenditure

84 Which one of the following is the most liquid asset?

    A   Land

    B   Trade receivables

    C   Inventory

    D   Savings account

85 A business has an average inventory holding period of 80 days, receives payment from its customers in 40 days and pays its payables in 45 days.

What is the working capital (cash operating) cycle, in days, for the business?

    A   120 days

    B   165 days

    C   75 days

    D   5 days

86 If a business increases its inventory holding period by 5 days and increases the time it takes to pay its payables by 7 days, what is the impact on the working capital cycle?

87 If a business increases its receivable collection period by 10 days and decreases its inventory holding period by 3 days, what is the impact on the working capital cycle (cash operating cycle)?

88 AP had a balance outstanding on trade receivables at 30 September 20X6 of £68,000. Forecast credit sales for the next six months are £250,000 and customers are expected to return goods with a sales value of £2,500.

Based on past experience, within the next six months AP expects to collect £252,100 cash and to write off, as irrecoverable debts, 5% of the balance outstanding at 30 September 20X6.

Calculate AP's forecast trade receivables days outstanding at 31 March 20X7.

89 KAI's trade receivables balance at 1 April 20X6 was £22,000. KAI's statement of profit or loss showed revenue from credit sales of £290,510 during the year ended 31 March 20X7.

KAI's trade receivables at 31 March 20X7 were 49 days.

Assume KAI's sales occur evenly throughout the year and that all balances outstanding at 1 April 20X6 have been received.

Also, it should be assumed all sales are on credit, there were no irrecoverable debts and no trade discount was given.

How much cash did KAI receive from its customers during the year to 31 March 20X7?

A £268,510

B £273,510

C £312,510

D £351,510

90 A company has annual sales of £4 million, annual cost of sales of £3 million and admin costs of £1.5 million. Its statement of financial position includes among assets and liabilities the following:

Trade receivables £400,000
Trade payables £300,000
Inventory £800,000

What is the company's working capital cycle?

91 DX has gathered the following information for the year ended 31 May 20X5.

	31 May 20X5
Gross profit	1,000,000
Trade receivables	290,000
Trade payables	190,000
Trade receivables collection period in days	44.1
Inventory holding period in days	93.9

(a) Complete the table below (round your answers to the nearest 10,000 where appropriate).

	31 May 20X5
Sales revenue	
Cost of sales	
Inventories level in the statement of financial position	
Trade payables payment period in days	

(b) The working capital cycle for DX is ☐ days

92 An extract from a company's trial balance at the end of its financial year is given below:

	£000
Sales revenue (85% on credit)	2,600
Cost of sales	1,800
Inventory of finished goods	220
Trade receivables	350
Trade payables	260

Calculate the following working capital ratios:

(i) Inventory holding period

(ii) Trade receivables collection period

(iii) Trade payables payment period

93 The following figures have been extracted from the financial statements of a company for the year ended December 20X3.

Statement of Financial Position (Extract)	£000	Statement of Profit or Loss (Extract)	£000
Inventories	150	Revenue	2,700
Receivables	300	Cost of sales	1,300
Cash	25	Gross profit	1,400
Payables	230	Admin costs	500
Overdraft	90	Distribution costs	350
Long term liabilities	1,400	Profit from operations	550
Equity	2,100	Finance cost	75
		Profit before tax	475
		Profit after tax	380

(a) Calculate the following (to the nearest day):

The inventory holding period is _____ days

The trade receivables collection period is _____ days

The trade payables payment period is _____ days

(b) Using your answers to part (b) calculate the cash operating cycle for the company.

The working capital cycle is _____ days

(c) Calculate the interest cover (to one decimal place).

The interest cover is _____ times

(d) Calculate the quick ratio (to one decimal place).

The quick ratio is _____

(e) Calculate the return on capital employed (ROCE) (to one decimal place).

The return on capital employed (ROCE) is _____ %

(f) Calculate the return on shareholders' funds (to one decimal place).

The return on shareholders' funds is _____ %

PRACTICE QUESTIONS : SECTION 1

94 BDQ's annual sales are £100m of which 95% are made on credit. Receivables at the beginning of the year were £10 million and at the end of the year they were £12 million. 10% of receivables were non-trade related.

What is BDQ's average collection period?

A   36.5 days

B   40 days

C   38 days

D   46 days

95 Complete the following sentences by selecting the correct options:

To improve the working capital cycle, a business could **[increase/decrease]** its debt collection period and/or **[extend/shorten]** the credit period it obtains from its suppliers.

96 In October, a company made credit purchases of £18,000 and credit sales of £24,000. All sales are made on the basis of cost plus 25%.

By how much will working capital increase in October as a result of these transactions?

97 A company has annual sales revenues of £30 million and the following working capital periods:

Inventory conversion period	2.5 months
Accounts receivable collection period	2.0 months
Accounts payable payment period	1.5 months

Production costs represent 70% of sales revenue.

Calculate the total amount held in working capital excluding cash and cash equivalents.

98 Select the correct options to complete the following sentences:

Over-capitalisation is a situation where a firm has **[more/less]** working capital than it needs. This often results in a business having a significant cash **[surplus/deficit]**.

99 HL has been trading profitably, but has recently been accused of overtrading.

(i) **Explain the consequences of overtrading, and explain what maybe be indicators that is overtrading.**

(ii) **Identify actions that HL could take to correct the problems of overtrading.**

RAISING FINANCE

INTEREST RATES

100 Which of the following best describes a capped rate of interest?

    A   Interest rate that is guaranteed not to exceed a specified level

    B   Interest rate that remains the same for the period of borrowing

    C   Interest charge that floats in line with bank base rates

    D   Interest rate that fluctuates in line with an agreed indicator

101 Which of the following best describes a fixed rate of interest?

    A   Interest rate that is guaranteed not to exceed a specified level

    B   Interest rate that remains the same for the period of borrowing

    C   Interest charge that floats in line with bank base rates

    D   Interest rate that fluctuates in line with an agreed indicator

102 Which of the following best describes a variable rate of interest?

    A   Interest rate that is guaranteed not to exceed a specified level

    B   Interest rate that remains the same for the period of borrowing

    C   Interest charge that floats in line with bank base rates

    D   Interest rate that fluctuates in line with an agreed indicator

103 What does APR stand for?

    A   Actual Percentage Rate

    B   Annual Percentage Rate

    C   Average Percentage Rate

    D   Annual Point Rate

104 What is the difference between a flat rate loan and an APR loan?

PRACTICE QUESTIONS : SECTION 1

FINANCING OPTIONS

105 Which one of the following best describes the main features of an overdraft?

    A   Interest rates are low; it is available for as long as required; it is useful for capital purchases

    B   Interest rates are low; it is repayable on demand; it is useful for capital purchases

    C   Interest rates are low; repayments can be negotiated; it is useful for capital purchases

    D   Interest rates are high; repayments can be negotiated; it is a short-term form of finance

    E   Interest rates are high; it is repayable on demand; it is a short-term form of finance

    F   Interest rates are high; it is available for as long as required; it is a long-term form of finance

106 Which one of the following best describes the main features of a bank loan?

    A   Interest rates are low; it is available for as long as required; it is useful for capital purchases

    B   Interest rates are low; it is repayable on demand; it is useful for capital purchases

    C   Interest rates are low; repayments can be negotiated; it is useful for capital purchases

    D   Interest rates are high; repayments can be negotiated; it is a short-term form of finance

    E   Interest rates are high; it is repayable on demand; it is a short-term form of finance

    F   Interest rates are high; it is available for as long as required; it is a long-term form of finance

107 A bank has offered to lend a company £60,000 to be repaid over one year in equal monthly instalments of £5,500. **What is the flat rate of interest being charged?**

108 **What is the annual flat rate of interest for a loan of £200,000 over 5 years if the monthly repayments are £4,000?**

109 A bank has offered to lend a company £100,000 to be repaid over 36 months in equal instalments. The flat rate of interest is 2%.

Calculate the monthly repayment of capital and interest.

AAT: CASH AND FINANCIAL MANAGEMENT

110 A company has arranged a bank overdraft facility of £50,000. It has the following terms:

- The current annual interest is 15%
- The interest is calculated on the closing monthly overdrawn balance and is included in the next month's opening balance
- Assume there are no differences in the monthly charges for the number of days in the month

Calculate the monthly interest costs to the nearest penny. Minus signs must be used to denote any bank overdraft and interest to be paid

	Month 3	Month 4	Month 5	Month 6	Month 7
Forecast net cash flow	7,500	−7,500	15,000	−15,000	−10,000
Opening balance	−5,000				
Closing balance before interest					
Overdraft interest to be charged					

111 A company invests £250,000 in shares of S Jack, a quoted company. S Jack has 20 million £1 shares in issue. The current market price of S Jack's share is £2.50. S Jack's operating profit in 20X2 was £15.41 million. The dividend paid to shareholders was 12p a share.

Calculate the dividend yield for S Jack.

112 Which of the following are types of security for borrowing?

(i) Floating charge

(ii) Fixed charge

(iii) Capped charge

(iv) Variable charge

A (i) and (ii)

B (iii) and (iv)

C (i), (ii) and (iv)

D (ii) and (iv)

113 Identify whether the following statements are true or false

Statement	True	False
A floating charge is security on a loan supplied by a group of assets		
A fixed charge is security on a loan supplied by a specific asset		
Gearing is calculated as total debt / (total debt + equity), where total debt = long and short term debt.		
Higher gearing indicates greater risk to lenders and investors		
Lower interest cover is less risky		

114 **(i)** A company has debt of £50,000, current assets of £10,000, share capital of £125,000 and share premium of £15,000. What is the gearing ratio?

    A   26.3%

    B   28.6%

    C   30.0%

    D   32.4%

(ii) A company has a bank loan of £1,200,000, an overdraft of £150,000 and trade payables of £200,000. Shareholder funds total £2,000,000. What is the gearing ratio?

    A   37.5%

    B   40.3%

    C   43.7%

    D   60.0%

115 Complete the sentences below by picking the correct options.

A bank loan is often **[less/more]** expensive than an overdraft, mainly due to the **[higher/lower]** interest rates.

An overdraft can be **[more expensive/cheaper]** overall, because we only borrow what's needed, on a daily basis.

116 The firm of Red & Bull is planning to expand its production facilities. The expansion plans will require the purchase of new machinery at a cost of £75,000 and a working capital injection of £34,000.

The partnership has been seeking possible means of funding the expansion and has been offered two options:

Option 1

A bank loan of £75,000 secured on the new machinery. Capital repayments are to be made over 3 years in equal, annual instalments. The interest rate is fixed at 8% per annum calculated on the capital balance outstanding at the beginning of each year.

An arrangement equal to 2% of the bank loan is payable at the beginning of the loan term.

The bank is also offering an overdraft facility up to £40,000 which attracts an annual interest rate of 20%. The partners believe that they will require an overdraft of £16,000 for nine months for the first year.

Option 2

A bank loan of £111,000 secured on the assets of the partnership. Principal (capital) repayments are to be made over 3 years, on a monthly basis.

The interest rate is fixed at 6% per annum for the first two years and will then revert to a variable interest rate set at 7% above the base rate. The interest charged is based on the amount outstanding at the start of each year.

An arrangement fee equal to 1% of the bank loan is payable at the beginning of the loan term.

Under this option there will be no requirement for a bank overdraft facility.

An extract from the partnership policy in respect of raising finance states the following:

- The maximum overdraft facility that the partnership may obtain is £20,000.
- Total costs are to be kept as low as possible.
- Loan finance may be secured on the assets of the partnership.
- The partners should not give personal guarantees or security for loan finance.

Complete the table below to calculate the total cost to the partnership for the first two years of financing under each options:

	Loan interest £	Capital repayments £	Arrangement fee £	Overdraft interest £	Total cost £
Option 1					
Option 2					

Based on these costs, and the partnership policy, which financing option should the partnership select? (Tick one.)

Option 1	
Option 2	

117 Bogstandard Brooms is experiencing difficulty in collecting its debts within the terms of 30 days which they offer. Its sales ledger balances total, on average, £500,000 which is equivalent to 60 days sales. The company has an overdraft facility of £750,000 on which it pays interest of 8% per annum. Because of the high level of receivables, the overdraft level is never less than £500,000.

Cashrich Credit plc have offered them a without recourse factoring arrangement whereby they will administer the sales ledger, pay 85% of the invoice value immediately it is issued and the balance when they are paid by the customer or 60 days later, whichever is the earlier. They will charge 2½% of the revenue which is estimated at £3,000,000 per annum.

You estimate that this will save administration costs of the sales ledger of £15,000 per annum.

Assuming that the customers will still pay after 60 days, will this be cost effective or not? Show your calculations.

118

Statement	True	False
Invoice discounting passes control of the sales ledger and credit control function to the invoice discounting company		

119 A company needs to acquire some new plant and is considering the most appropriate means of funding the purchase. The purchase price is £400,000.

Prepare notes describing the following financing options; include the implications of each option on:

- the financial position of the company
- the gearing of the company

    1   Hire purchase agreement for 5 years

    2   Lease with a minimum term of 6 years

    3   Issue of equity shares

    4   Taking out a bank loan

    5   Funding using bonds

    6   Debt factoring

120 Explain the differences between a normal lease and a short term or low value item lease.

121 A business requires a loan of £50,000 to re-equipment the machinery department.

There are 2 different loans available with different monthly repayment plans.

Option 1

- 1 payment of £2,500
- 60 payments of £800
- Final payment of £2,000

Option 2

- 1 payment of £2,500
- 30 payments of £1,750

What is the interest cost (in £ and %) of each option and which one should the business opt for?

122 A company intends to raise capital of £1.5 million to purchase a non-current asset. The following are option available to raise the finance required:

Option 1

- Bank loan of £1.5 million borrowed over 18 months
- Flat rate interest charged on the initial balance of 8%
- Arrangement fee of 2% of the initial loan payable in the first month

Option 2

- Hire purchase agreement for the non-current asset purchase of £1.5 million
- Total interest payable is £152,793
- 17 regular monthly payments
- Option to purchase in the last month at an extra cost of £91,836
- The term is 18 months with an APR of 12.5%

Option 3

- Lease agreement for the non-current asset of £1.5 million
- Monthly payments will be £104,167

What is the monthly and total cash flow of each option?

123 A company wishes to borrow £300,000 to finance the purchase of new hi-tech printing machine. They expect to repay the borrowing over 90 months.

Three options have been identified.

Option 1	Bank loan repaid in 90 monthly instalments. Interest rate: 8.0% APR	Administration charge: £1,500	Monthly repayment: £4,444
Option 2	Bank loan repaid in 30 equal quarterly instalments. Interest rate: 5.0% per annum flat rate.	Administration charge: £1,000	
Option 3	Bank overdraft facility of £300,000 which will be reviewed every year when the administration fee is paid. Interest rate: 11% per annum	Annual administration fee: £800 at the start of each year	

In all options, the administration charge/fee is paid on the first day of the loan and if appropriate, on the anniversary of the loan and does not form part of the monthly repayment.

(a) How much interest and administration charge will be paid is option 1 is taken?

(b) How much interest and administration charge will be paid if option 2 is taken?

(c) How much is the quarterly repayment for option 2?

If option 3 is taken, the company expects to have an average overdraft of £150,000 over 7 and a half years. This amount should be used as the basis to calculate the interest charged on the overdraft.

(d) How much interest and administration fee will be paid if option 3 is taken?

124 A company's year end is 31st March 20X7

The company has taken out a 6 year bank loan on 30th September 20X5. The principle amount is £1,500,000 and is being repaid in equal monthly instalments.

In the year ending 31st March 20X6 £39,750 was paid in interest. In the year ending 31st March 20X7 £67,500 was paid in interest.

(a) Complete the accounting entry which would have been made on the day the loan was received.

Account	Debit	Credit	Amount £
Current bank account			
Current loan account			
Long-term loan account			

Below is the trial balance that will be used to prepare the company's financial statements as at 31st March 20X7

(b) Complete the missing figures. Round your answer to the nearest £000

Extract of the Trial balance	31st March 20X7	31st March 20X6
Plant and machinery	8,000	6,300
Inventories	3,000	2,500
Trade receivables	2,100	2,100
Bank current account	60	(60)
Trade payable	(5,700)	(5,100)
Other creditors	(1,900)	(1,600)
Current portion of long term loan		
Long term loan		
Retained profit	(4,900)	(3,300)
Share capital	(500)	(500)
Turnover	(59,700)	(57,600)
Purchases	43,600	42,700
Other operating costs	13,300	12,600
Long term loan interest		
Taxation	1,200	1,200

(c) Calculate the gearing and interest cover for both years. Round your answer to the nearest whole percent.

	20X7	20X6
Gearing	%	%

125 A company intends to raise capital of £1 million (£1m) to purchase a non-current asset. After considering many possibilities; they have narrowed their options down to the following:

Option 1

The company takes out a bank loan for £1m for two years, with interest chargeable at 6% per annum on the initial loan and an arrangement fee of 12.5% of the total interest payable on the loan. The agreed terms of the loan are that the interest is charged on a flat rate on the initial balance of £1m

Option 2

The company has a large balance of outstanding trade receivables and the credit control department is having little success in obtaining the outstanding debt from these customers. The company has been approached by a debt factoring company to purchase some of these trade receivables to the value of £1.25m from the company for £1m by entering into a factoring arrangement.

Option 3

Rather than purchase the non-current asset, the company chooses to lease it instead for two years with lease rental payments of £625,000 per annum.

The finance director has asked you to prepare a report for each option, including the cost to the company together with its advantages and disadvantages. The report should also include the treatment of each option in the financial statements and how they affect the company's liquidity, gearing and credit rating.

126 A company is considering the use of without recourse factoring to manage its trade receivables.

It currently has a balance outstanding on trade receivables of £180,000 and annual sales revenue of £1,095,000. It anticipates that this level of sales revenue and trade receivables will continue for at least the next year. It estimates that the use of the factoring company will result in a reduction in credit control costs of £20,000 per annum.

The factoring company will charge a fee of 2.5% of all invoiced sales. It will give an advance of 90% of invoiced sales and charge interest at a rate of 12% per annum.

Calculate the annual cost of factoring net of credit control cost savings?

A   £26,815

B   £46,815

C   £98,260

D   £118,260

127 A company is looking to improve its cash flow and has been considering various finance products. The company has a balance on its sales ledger of £1,250,145 as at the 31 July 20X3.

A finance company has offered to provide a facility where the company can borrow up to £750,000 or a maximum of 80% of the total outstanding sales ledger balance. The finance company administers the sales ledger on behalf of the company for a fee of £1,500 per month.

The maximum amount available to borrow at the 31 July 20X3 is:

£ _____

128 **Invoice discounting is a method where:**

    A   Discounts are given for early payment of invoices

    B   A finance house lends money against invoices issued

    C   A reduction is given for faulty goods

    D   A judgement given by a court

129 Spruce Ltd is considering methods to speed up receipts from credit customers and has been offered a without-recourse factoring arrangement.

Which of the following is NOT likely to be an advantage of such an agreement?

    A   Insurance against irrecoverable debts

    B   Improved relationship with customers

    C   Managers can spend more time running the company rather than credit control

    D   Reduced overdraft

130 Select true or false for the following statements about crowdfunding:

	True	False
Crowdfunding obtains funding from a few wealthy investors		
Crowdfunding is most common with start-up and smaller businesses		
Crowdfunding uses technology and online platforms to attract investors		
Crowdfunding is arranged with a bank		
Crowdfunding can also boost brand awareness and help build a customer base		
Large listed businesses often use crowdfunding		

AAT: CASH AND FINANCIAL MANAGEMENT

INVESTING SURPLUS FUNDS

131 KIT has £1 million to invest for one year. It can lock it away at a fixed rate of 7% for the full year, or invest at 6.5% for a three-month term, speculating on an increase in interest rates. Assume that the rate available increases to 7.5% after three months, and that KIT invests at this rate for the rest of the year.

By how much is KIT better off from its gamble on interest rates?

- A £2,500
- B £12,836
- C £73,414
- D £3,414

132 A company has £500,000 surplus cash to be invested for 10 months only. There are two options available:

1 Place the money in a deposit account earning 3% interest per annum. There are no restrictions on withdrawal. Interest is paid annually on the anniversary of the opening of the account and on the day of closure of the account.

2 Place the money in a deposit account earning 5% interest per annum, providing the funds are not withdrawn before 12 months. The penalty of withdrawal is a loss of 3 months interest.

Answer the following questions based on the information

(a) How much interest is earned if option 1 is chosen?

(b) How much interest is earned if option 2 is chosen?

133 Calculate the interest yield (to 2 decimal places) on 5.3% Treasury Stock 20X4 with a current market price of £105.

134 An issue of 6% Treasury Stock 20X2 has taken place. The nominal value is £100. A company has purchased £150,000 worth of Gilts at a price of £175,000.

Calculate how much interest the company will receive for each six month period and the interest yield (to two decimal places)

135 A company has £800,000 invested in a one year fixed interest bond which pays 4.5% per annum. The company is going to have with draw the full amount from the investment in the 10th month of investment. The penalty for early redemption is the loss of one month's interest.

Calculate the total amount of interest that the company will receive.

136 Explain THREE factors that a company should consider before deciding how to invest short term cash surpluses.

PRACTICE QUESTIONS : SECTION 1

137 A company invests £54,000 in a fixed interest deposit account for three years. The rate of interest is 8.6%.

Calculate the balance in the account after three years if the interest is paid annually at the end of each year and the interest received remains in the account (to 2 decimal places).

138 An investment has an interest rate of 2.9% above the base rate of 0.5%.

If £20,000 is invested what will be the value of the investment in one year's time?

139 How much will an investor need to invest for one year to earn £2,500 interest, assuming a fixed annual rate of interest of 2%?

140 Select the correct options to complete the following sentences:

Certificates of deposit are certificates issued by **[banks/companies/stock exchange/local authority]** that certify that an amount of money has been deposited and will be repaid at a specific date in the future. They **[can/cannot]** be traded on a market. They are considered to be a **[low risk/high risk]** investment.

Local authority short-term loans are certificates issued by **[banks/companies/stock exchange/local authorities]** and backed by the government. They **[can/cannot]** be traded on a market. They are considered to be a **[low risk bank loan/high risk bank loan/low risk investment/high risk investment]**.

Government securities are also known as **[gold-edged/gilt-edged/gilted]** securities and **[can/cannot]** be traded. Interest rates are **[fixed/variable]** and these types of securities are considered to be **[low risk/high risk]** because they **[are/are not]** backed by the government.

Bank deposit accounts tend to have a **[lower/higher]** return than shares, as they are much **[lower/higher]** risk. They tend to have **[lower/higher]** interest rates than gilts and debentures as they are a **[more/less]** liquid investment.

Shares are issued by **[banks/companies/stock exchange/local authorities]** and **[can/cannot]** be traded. Dividends are usually **[fixed/variable]**. Shares are considered to be a **[low risk/high risk]** investment. This is because the returns from shares are **[fixed/sometime volatile]** and the value of the investment is **[stable/uncertain]**.

141 A company has £9,000 to invest. It is going to buy 4% treasury stock. The interest receivable on the stock will be £600 in the year.

What is the market price of the stock?

142 A company is going to make a dividend pay-out of £640,000. The share capital is £800,000 with a nominal value of £0.50 per share.

What is the dividend payable per share?

143 A company is going to pay a dividend of £3 per share. The current market price is £30.50 per share.

What is the dividend yield per share (2 decimal places)?

144 An investor bought 5,000 shares when the share price was £1.25 per share. The shares were sold eight months later at a gross profit of £750.

What was the selling price per share?

145 The investment manual of a treasury department in a large company has the following policy for investing surplus funds:

- The investment must be convertible to cash within 45 days.
- The maximum amount to be invested in any one type of investment is £20,000.
- The interest rate must be at least 3% above base rate which is currently 1%.
- The investment must not include shares.
- Only low or medium risk investments are to be selected.

Four possible investment options are available:

Option 1

Investment of £20,000 required; 90 – day notice period; medium risk; investment portfolio includes shares; interest rate is 5% per annum.

Option 2

Maximum investment is £40,000 and minimum investment is £3,000; 30 – day notice period; interest rate is 4.5%; low risk; does not include investment in shares.

Option 3

Investment portfolio comprises stocks and shares; high risk; projected interest rate is 7% and a minimum investment of £40,000 is required; 40 – day notice period.

Option 4

Low risk; guaranteed return of 3% per annum; no stocks or shares; minimum investment of £52,000; 7 – day notice period.

Complete the table below, by typing either yes or no into each cell, to show which of the policy requirements are met by each of the options.

	Convertible within 45 days	Investment £20,000 or below	Interest rate 3% above base	Investment does not include shares	Low or Medium Risk
Option 1					
Option 2					
Option 3					
Option 4					

The company should select **[Option 1/Option 2/Option 3/Option 4/none of the options]**.

146 A company has surplus funds to invest for a period of 3 months. It is considering potential investment opportunities as follows:

Investment 1

Purchase treasury bills issued by the country's central bank. The treasury bills can be purchased now for a period of 91 days. The purchase price is £995 per £1,000.

Investment 2

Invest in a 30 day notice bank deposit account. The account will pay a variable rate of interest of 2.5% per annum, payable quarterly.

Compare and contrast the investment options. Your answer should include relevant calculations.

147 DH raised cash through an equity share issue to pay for a new factory it planned to construct. However, the factory contract has been delayed and payments are not expected to be required for three or four months. DH is going to invest its surplus funds until they are required.

One of the directors of DH has identified three possible investment opportunities:

(i) Treasury bills issued by the central bank of DH's country. They could be purchased on 1 December 20X6 for a period of 91 days. The likely purchase price is £990 per £1,000.

(ii) Equities quoted on DH's local stock exchange. The stock exchange has had a good record in recent months with the equity index increasing in value for 14 consecutive months. The director recommends that DH invests in three large multinational entities, each paying an annual dividend that provides an annual yield of 10% on the current share price.

(iii) DH's bank would pay 3.5% per year on money placed in a deposit account with 30 days' notice.

Prepare notes on the risk and effective yield of each of the above investment opportunities.

148 The table below identifies the main features of four different investment opportunities:

	Minimum investment	Maximum investment	Includes shares	Notice period	% return	Risk
Option 1	£45,000	£60,000	Yes	90 days	3% variable	Medium
Option 2	£25,000	£75,000	No	30 days	2% variable	Low
Option 3	£30,000	£100,000	Yes	40 days	7% fixed	High
Option 4	£53,000	£70,000	No	7 days	3.5% fixed	Low

The general trend is that interest rates are decreasing and this trend is expected to continue for the foreseeable future.

Identify which of the investment options are appropriate in each of the situation described below (there may be more than one suitable option)

	Suitable options
A partnership has £50,000 to invest	
An investing organisation requires a low risk investment	
A guaranteed interest rate of 3% is required	
The notice period needs to be less than 50 days	
The investment should not include shares	

AAT: CASH AND FINANCIAL MANAGEMENT

149 A company has £250,000 surplus cash and the treasurer estimates that the cash is free to be invested for up to three years.

Write a report which considers the risk, return and liquidity of each of the following investment options:

- Land
- Long term bank deposit account
- Shares in a public company
- Certificates of deposit
- Treasury bills

150 A company has £550,000 surplus cash to be invested.

Write a report to the Finance Director discussing the options described below. Consider the potential return, the risks and any other issues that should be considered. You should conclude on which investment the company should invest in.

Option 1

A four year fixed rate bond with a High Street bank paying interest of 6% per annum

Option 2

A business is looking to expand and is asking for help financing this expansion. The company is selling shares at £10 per share. The expansion will create new jobs in an area of unemployment.

Option 3

Invest in an oil mine. Shares are £15 each. Research shows that oil is in abundance but there are rumours of child labour and health and safety issue surrounding the mine's owners.

151 The table below lists the assets in a portfolio of investments held by a company

Investment	Value £000	Expected return %
1	1,500	5.0
2	5,000	8.0
3	1,000	2.5
4	750	1.2
Total	8,250	

(a) Calculate the percentage expected return for the portfolio. Show your answer to one decimal place.

The manager of the portfolio has cashed in investment 3.

(b) Calculate the revised percentage expected return for the now reduced portfolio. Show you answer to one decimal place.

152 A company has £4,000,000 surplus cash to be invested for five years. The Finance Director has been tasked with preparing a board paper for discussion at the next board meeting. He/she/they has delegated this task to you as the Treasury Accountant.

The options are as follows:

1   A current account paying 0.4% interest per annum. Minimum investment £1.

2   A fixed rate account with a high street bank paying 2.4% interest per annum. Minimum investment £250,000.

3   A 90-day notice deposit account paying 1.1% interest per annum. Minimum investment £50,000.

4   Purchase 3% Treasury Stock with a redemption date in five years' time for the full £4,000,000 in £100 blocks. The nominal value of each block is £100.

5   Purchase £4,000,000 worth of Certificates of Deposit from a reputable UK bank in £1,000 blocks with an interest rate of 4% and a term of five years.

Write a report to the Finance Director outlining the terms and conditions of each option, together with the amount of income earned. Your answer should include brief comments on the risk, return and liquidity of each option and give a recommendation as to which option the company should select.

153 A company has £250,000 surplus cash to be invested It believes that this money will not be required for two years, however the industry can be unpredictable and cash flows have been historically volatile.

Write a report to the Finance Director discussing the options described below. Consider the potential return, the risks and any other issues that should be considered.

Option 1

Invest in a local piece of land.

Option 2

A 30 day notice savings account with the company's bank paying 1% per annum.

Option 3

Invest the funds in gold bars, which will be stored safely at the bank

Option 4

Invest in 4% Treasury bonds that are redeemable in three years' time.

154 **If investors require a return of 5% what should the market price be of 3% £100 nominal value irredeemable bonds?**

155 A company makes an investment of £18,000 and receives interest of £200 per month and then is repaid a total of £19,500 in a year's time.

What is the rate of interest / annual return on this investment (1 decimal places)?

IMPACT OF REGULATIONS AND POLICIES ON FINANCING AND INVESTMENT

GOVERNMENT POLICY AND REGULATIONS

156 (i) What is Quantitative Easing and why might it be used?

(ii) What is the main reason why governments would not normally consider using quantitative easing to boost economic growth?

A It would result in the government having to increase taxes to pay for it.

B It would generate high inflationary pressure.

C It would result in excessive savings, thus creating a leakage in the economy.

D It would crowd out private investment

157 Complete this sentence:

Central banks (e.g. The Bank of England) try to increase the amount of lending and activity in the economy indirectly, by **lowering/raising** interest rates. **Lower/higher** interest rates encourage people to spend, not save.

158 What are the two main policies that Governments use to control the supply of money, interest rates and the availability of credit? What are these policies?

(i)

(ii)

159 Which of the following points apply to a business investing in a local economy, and which apply to investing in a wider/global economy?

Statement	Local economy	Global economy
Online selling, either through a business's own website or via a platform such as Ebay or Amazon Marketplace allows easy access to this economy		
Brand awareness amongst potential customers will likely be higher in this economy		
This economy usually has the potential for faster and larger growth		
A business is likely to have better knowledge of customer tastes and competitors in this economy		
There is likely to be increased delivery, regulatory and legal costs if expanding into this economy		
Investing in this economy is generally more risky for a business		

160 Which one of the following is the Bank of England responsible for?

- A   Setting the APR for banks
- B   Setting short term interest rates
- C   Setting the corporation tax rate
- D   Setting the VAT rate

161 Monetary policy is a process where a central bank

- A   increases or decreases the supply of gilts
- B   increase or decreases the value of loans to businesses
- C   increases of decreases the rates of tax on businesses
- D   increases or decreases the supply of money

162 Tick if the following statements are true or false

Statement	True	False
The Bribery Act covers all aspects of white collar crime		
Suspected money laundering of amounts under £500 do not need to be reported		
Companies Act required a company to disclose political donations it makes		
Companies Act requires directors to consider how a company's actions impact the environment and employees as well as shareholders		
Money laundering regulations only cover accountants		

Section 2

ANSWERS TO PRACTICE QUESTIONS

CASH AND PROFIT

TYPES OF CASH FLOW

1

Description	Type of receipt or payment
Proceeds from the disposal of non-current assets	Capital receipts
Buy new factory	Capital payment
Customer paying their debt	Regular revenue receipt
Pay legal fee due to product complaints	Exceptional payment
Unexpected tax refund	Exceptional receipt
Payment of wages	Regular revenue expense
Pay corporation tax for the year	Payment to HM Revenue and Customs
Payments made to the owners of the business	Drawings

CASH ADJUSTMENTS

2 (a) **Trade receivables**

	£		£
Opening balance	10,500	Cash received	297,600
Sales	300,000	Closing balance	12,900
	310,500		310,500

(b) **Rent**

	£		£
Opening prepayment	750	Statement of profit or loss	6,000
Cash paid	6,250	Closing prepayment	1,000
	7,000		7,000

(c) **Payroll expenses**

	£		£
Cash paid	22,000	Opening accrual	200
Closing accrual	320	Statement of profit or loss	22,120
	22,320		22,320

(d) **Trade payables**

	£		£
Cash paid	149,500	Opening balance	5,800
Closing balance	6,300	Purchases	150,000
	155,800		155,800

3   B

	£
Purchases on credit	360,000
Increase in trade payables	15,000
Therefore payments to suppliers	345,000

An increase in trade payables means that the company is buying more on credit that they are paying back to their suppliers, for example:

Trade payables

	£		£
Cash paid	**345,000**	Opening balance	6,000
Closing balance 6,000 + 15,000	21,000	Purchases	360,000
	366,000		366,000

Changes in inventory levels have no effect on expected cash payments.

4   £15,900

Receivables

	£		£
B/f	70,000	Returns	2,000
Sales	200,000	Cash	250,000
		Irrecoverable debts (70,000 × 0.03)	2,100
		C/f	15,900
	270,000		270,000

ANSWERS TO PRACTICE QUESTIONS : SECTION 2

5 (a) £252,000

	£
Budgeted sales	240,000
Expected decrease in receivables	12,000
	252,000

The reduction in receivables means that the company will expect to receive more cash next month than the total of its credit sales for the month, for example:

Trade receivables

	£		£
Opening balance	20,000	Cash received	**252,000**
Sales	240,000	Closing balance 20,000 – 12,000	8,000
	260,000		260,000

Changes in inventory levels have no effect on expected cash receipts.

(b)

Item	Cash	Profit	Cash and profit
Depreciation on a machine		X	
Selling a non-current asset for its carry value of £1,500	X		
Repaying a bank loan	X		
Prepaying next year's rent	X		
Making a cash sale			X

6 (a) Disposals

	£		£
Original cost	12,000	Accumulated depreciation	5,250
		Loss on disposal	1,750
		Cash received	5,000
	12,000		12,000

(b) Disposals

	£		£
Original cost	500	Accumulated depreciation	300
Gain on disposal	75	Cash received	275
	575		575

KAPLAN PUBLISHING

(c) **Disposals**

	£		£
Original cost	12,000	Accumulated depreciation	5,856
		Loss on disposal	2,644
		Part-exchange	3,500
	12,000		12,000

Total cost − part-exchange value = cash paid for new vehicle
13,500 − 3,500 = £10,000

7

	Workings	£
Sales receipts	3,520 + 51,000 − 12,400	42,120
Purchases payments	400 + 26,000 − 3,004	23,396
Wages paid	As per SOPL	12,900
Advertising fees	1,200 + 2,010 − 800	2,410
Van expenses	110 + 3,069 − 80	3,099
Van depreciation	Non-cash	0

8

	Workings	£
Sales receipts	13,520 + 351,000 − 31,000	333,520
Purchases payments	4,400 + 126,000 − 8,000	122,400
Wages paid	As per SOPL	32,900
Electricity and van expenses paid	1,200 + 22,010 + 23,069 − 2,100	44,179
Phone expenses	12,567 − 80	12,487

9

	Workings	£
Rent paid	12,650 − 1,200 − 1,200	10,250
Office expenses	370 + 6,640 − 441	6,569
Printing expenses	567 + 17,118 − 3,655	14,030

10 (a) Calculate the cash received from receivables for the year ended 31 March 20x7.

	£		£
Credit sales	29,200	CASH	25,800
		Balance c/f	3,400
	29,200		29,200

ANSWERS TO PRACTICE QUESTIONS : SECTION 2

(b) Calculate the cash paid to payables for the year ended 31 March 20X7.

	£		£
CASH	8,840	Purchases	11,200
Discounts received	1,165		
Balance c/f	1,195		
	11,200		11,200

(c) Calculate the cash paid for rent for the year ended 31 March 20X7.

	£		£
CASH	4,500	Prepayment	900
		Rent for the year	3,600
	4,500		4,500

(d) Calculate the cash paid for general expenses for the year ended 31 March 20X7.

3 months' electricity =	£135
Accrual needs to be for 2 months, therefore:	
Accrual = £135 × 2/3 =	£90
General expenses	£1,840
Less accrual	£90
Cash	**£1,750**

11

	Workings	£
Operating profit		10,520
Change in inventory	£1,200 – £1,000 reduction in balance therefore increase in cash	200
Change in receivables	£10,000 – £7,650 reduction in balance therefore increase in cash	2,350
Change in payables	Closing balance = 1,200 + 2,400 – 2,000 = £1,600 £1,200 – £1,600 increase in balance therefore increase in cash	400
Adjustment for non-cash items	Depreciation charge	250
Purchase of non-current assets	£24,000 + £250 – £20,000 = £4,250 for additions	(4,250)
Tax paid	£2,600 + £2,700 – £2,800 = £2,500 paid	(2,500)
Net change in cash position		6,970
Cash position 1 May		30,000
Forecast cash position 31 July		36,970

KAPLAN PUBLISHING

12

	Workings	£
Operating profit		250,000
Change in inventory	No change	0
Change in receivables	£108,000 – £100,000 increase in balance therefore reduction in cash	(8,000)
Change in payables	Closing balance = 50,000 + 200,000 – 230,000 = £20,000 £50,000 – £20,000 reduction in balance therefore reduction in cash	(30,000)
Adjustment for non-cash items	Depreciation charge	25,000
Purchase of non-current assets	£25,000 + £24,000 – £20,000 = £29,000 additions £29,000 – £15,000 (leased asset) = £14,000 cash Plus £625 × 10 = £6,250 lease payments	(20,250)
Tax paid	£50,000 + £52,500 – £55,000 = £47,500 paid	(47,500)
Net change in cash position		169,250
Cash position 1 January 20X6		70,000
Forecast cash position 31 December 20X6		239,250

13 Style Limited's statement of profit or loss for the year ended 31 March 20X5

	£000
Revenue	8,210
Cost of sales (W1)	(3,937)
Gross profit	4,273
Administrative expenses	(1,540)
Distribution costs	(1,590)
Operating profit	1,143
Finance cost (1,500 × 6%)	(90)
Profit before tax	1,053
Income tax expense (250 + 100)	(350)
Profit for the period	703

Workings:

(W1) Cost of sales

	£000
Cost of goods	3,463
Add depreciation – buildings (W2)	96
– plant and equipment (W3)	348
Short term lease (W4)	30
	3,937

(W2) Buildings

	£000
Land and building at cost	5,190
Less: value of land	(2,000)
	3,190
Depreciation for year 3,190 × 3%	96

(W3) Plant and equipment

	£000
Plant and equipment cost	3,400
Less: Accumulated Depreciation	(1,659)
	1,741
Depreciation for year 1,741 × 20%	348

(W4) Short term lease

As the lease is for 12 months or less then the lease payments are simply expensed over the length of the lease

	£000
Total payments (£18,000 + 9m × £4,000pm)	54
This equates to 54/9 = £6,000 per month of the lease	
Apportioned to the 5 months in y/e 31 March X5 (£6,000 per month × 5 months)	30

14

Ruby and Daughters

Statement of profit or loss for the year

	£	£
Sales (W1)		44,000
Opening inventory	5,000	
Purchases (W2)	23,000	
Less: Closing inventory	(6,000)	
Cost of sales		(22,000)
Gross profit		22,000
Wages and salaries	20,800	
Rent (W3)	4,700	
Sundry expenses (W4)	250	
Depreciation (W5)	10,000	
		(35,750)
Net profit/(loss)		(13,750)

Workings:

(W1) **Sales ledger control account**

	£		£
Opening balance	12,000	Cash received from customers	40,000
Sales	44,000	Closing balance	16,000
	56,000		56,000

(W2) **Purchase ledger control account**

	£		£
Payments made to suppliers	25,000	Opening balance	7,000
Closing balance	5,000	Purchases	23,000
	30,000		30,000

(W3) **Rent account**

	£		£
Bank account	5,000	Statement of profit or loss	4,700
		Closing prepayment	300
	5,000		5,000

ANSWERS TO PRACTICE QUESTIONS : SECTION 2

(W4)   **Sundry expenses**

	£		£
Cash account	200	Statement of profit or loss	250
Closing accrual	50		
	250		250

(W5) **Depreciation**

Depreciation charge (50,000 × 20%) = £10,000

Debit	Depreciation expense (statement of profit or loss)	£10,000
Credit	Accumulated depreciation (SFP)	£10,000

15

Extract of the cash budget	**Period 4**
	£000
Receipts of cash sales	760 × 10% = 76
Receipts from trade receivables	445 + (760 × 90%) – 423 = 706
Receipt from disposal of non-current asset	930 – 60 – 3 – 858 = 9
Car lease payments	6 + 13 – 5 = (14)

FORECASTING

MOVING AVERAGES

Note: In the exam 'greyed out' boxes may no longer appear in which case zeros will need to be input to gain full marks.

16 (a)

	Sales volume (units)	Trend	Monthly variation
May	61,600		
June	39,100	52,000	–12,900
July	55,300	55,500	–200
August	72,100	59,000	13,100
September	49,600	62,500	–12,900
October	65,800	66,000	–200
November	82,600	69,500	13,100
December	60,100		

(b)

	Forecast trend	Variation	Forecast sales volume	Forecast sales £	Forecast purchases £
January	76,500	–200	76,300	1,106,350	331,905

17 (a)

	Sales volume (units)	Trend	Monthly variation
January	19,906		
February	22,390		
March	20,555	20,570	−15
April	18,666	20,620	−1,954
May	21,333	20,670	663
June	20,156	20,720	−564
July	22,640	20,770	1,870
August	20,805	20,820	−15
September	18,916	20,870	−1,954
October	21,583		
November	20,406		

(b)

	Forecast trend	Variation	Forecast sales volume	Forecast sales £	Forecast purchases £
December	21,020	1,870	22,890	686,700	192,276

18 (a)

	Sales volume (units)	Trend	Monthly variation % (2 d.p.)
October	6,408		
November	8,816	8,303	106.18% or 6.18%
December	9,686	8,479	114.24% or 14.24%
January	6,934	8,713	79.58% or −20.42%
February	9,520	8,965	106.19% or 6.19%
March	10,440	9,140	114.22% or 14.22%
April	7,460	9,375	79.57% or −20.43%
May	10,225		

Note: In the exam it will be clear which answer is required.

(b) The average monthly trend (to the nearest whole number) is 214

ANSWERS TO PRACTICE QUESTIONS : **SECTION 2**

19 (a)

Sales of footballs increase when the world cup is on.	
Sales of greetings cards increase in December.	✓
Sales of milk remain constant all year.	
Sales of houses increase in Spring.	✓
Sales of newspapers rise whenever it rains.	

(b)

Tennis rackets sales increase during Wimbledon.	
Over summer, more hosepipes are sold.	
Sales of raincoats increase in April.	
During the last general election, sales of ice-cream increased.	
Sales of diet books reach a peak after every Olympics.	✓

(c) A seasonal variation is a change in sales which occurs **at regular intervals, normally of less than a year** whereas a cyclical variation occurs **over a long time period.**

The underlying sales trend is the sales level excluding **all variations**.

20 (a)

Sales of houses increase when the England cricket team wins.	
Sales of wrapping paper increase in November and December.	✓
Sales of venetian blinds have been falling consistently for 3 years.	
Sales of wallpaper increase at the same time that sales of toothpaste fall.	
Sales of shoes rise in the summer.	✓

(b)

Tennis rackets sales decrease when it rains.	
Over summer, more ice creams are sold.	
Sales of gloves increase in Autumn.	
When Sky HD was launched a carpet firm in Cardiff experienced 20% sales growth.	
Over the last 50 years the average price of oil has increased for 5 years, then decreased for 5 years. This pattern continued over the 50 year period.	✓

MARK-UP AND MARGIN

21 (a) £900/100 × 140 = £1,260

(b) £900/60 × 100 = £1,500

22 (a)

	Sales volume (units)	Trend	Monthly variation
February	10,100		
March	10,950	10,900	50
April	11,650	11,200	450
May	11,000	11,500	–500
June	11,850	11,800	50
July	12,550	12,100	450
August	11,900	12,400	–500
September	12,750		

The monthly variation in July is **450** units.

(b)

	Forecast trend	Variation	Forecast sales volume	Forecast sales £
October	13,000	450	13,450	289,175

(c) £289,175 × 80% = £231,340

(d) £289,175/125 × 100 = £231,340

23

	Manufacturing	Sales	External
20X0			
January	230	× 1.05 = 241.50	× 1.1 = 265.65
February	140	× 1.05 = 147.00	× 1.1 = 161.70
March	132	× 1.05 = 138.60	× 1.1 = 152.46
January	51	n/a	÷ 93 × 100 = 54.84
February	60	n/a	÷ 93 × 100 = 64.52
March	18	n/a	÷ 93 × 100 = 19.35
		Total monthly sales value	**718.52**

ANSWERS TO PRACTICE QUESTIONS : SECTION 2

INDEXING

24

Month	1	2	3	4	5	6	7
Price	0.12	0.15	0.21	0.32	0.26	0.25	0.30
Index	57.14	71.43	100	152.38	123.8	119.05	142.86

Month 1 = 0.12 ÷ 0.21 × 100 = 57.14

Month 7 = 0.30 ÷ 0.21 × 100 = 142.86

25 C

£20,500 ÷ 131 × 151 = £23,630

26 C

Current cost = £5 × 430 ÷ 150

27 A

(£2,000 × 120 ÷ 160) = £1,500

28 (a)

Period	1	2	3	4	5
Sales price (£)	40.00	55.00	40/80 × 120 = 60.00	48.00	40/80 × 121= 60.50
Index	80.00	80/40 × 55 = 110.00	120.00	80/40 × 48 = 96.00	121.00

(b) 40.00 ÷ 100 × 80 = £32.00

29 (a)

Month	Purchases volume (tonnes)	Trend	Monthly variation
1	5,150		
2	5,241	5,293	−52
3	5,487	5,448	39
4	5,615	5,461	154
5	5,280	5,450	−170
6	5,456	5,461	−5
7	5,648	5,665	−17
8	5,890	5,662	228
9	5,448	5,676	−228
10	5,689	5,661	28
11	5,847	5,845	2
12	6,000		

(b) (5,845 − 5,293) ÷ 9 = 61 tonnes

KAPLAN PUBLISHING

AAT: CASH AND FINANCIAL MANAGEMENT

(c)

Month 17 (tonnes)	Month 18 (tonnes)
6,211	6,272

(d) 6,272 × £56 × 142 ÷ 125 = £398,999.55 = £399,000 rounded

REGRESSION ANALYSIS

30 Orders = 100,000 + (30 × 240) = 107,200

Orders adjusted for seasonal index = [100,000 + (30 × 240)] × 1.08 = 115,776

Overhead cost = £10,000 + (£0.25 × 115,776) = £38,944

Answer is £39,000

31 We have been given the trend equation. We need to plug in the value for x so that we can find y.

X is the time period reference number and for the first quarter of year 1 is 1. The time period reference number for the third quarter of year 7 is 27. (Just keep adding 1 to the time period reference number for each new quarter, thus quarter 2, year 1, x = 2; quarter 3, year 1, x = 3; quarter 4, year 1, x = 4; quarter 1, year 2, x = 5, etc.)

y = 25,000 + 6,500 × 27 = 200,500 units

This is the trend we now need to multiply by the seasonal variation for quarter 3:

Forecast = 200,500 × 150/100 = 300,750 units.

32 D

Quarter	Value of x		Trend units			Forecast sales units
1	25	y = (26 × 25) + 8,850	9,500	× 85%	=	8,075
2	26	y = (26 × 26) + 8,850	9,526	× 95%	=	9,050
3	27	y = (26 × 27) + 8,850	9,552	× 105%	=	10,030
4	28	y = (26 × 28) + 8,850	9,578	× 115%	=	11,015
						38,170

Difference between Q1 and Q4 budgeted sales = 11,015 – 8,075 = 2,940 units

33 D

Since no inventories are held, budgeted production will be equal to budgeted sales.

Budgeted production each quarter = 38,170/4 = 9,542.5 units

34

Quarter	Trend sales units	Actual sales units	Variation units
1	13,000	14,000	+1,000
2	16,000	18,000	+2,000
3	19,000	18,000	−1,000
4	22,000	20,000	−2,000

Year 2 Quarter 1 = 10,000 + (3,000 × 5) = 25,000 + 1,000 = 26,000 units

Year 2 Quarter 2 = 10,000 + (3,000 × 6) = 28,000 + 2,000 = 30,000 units

Year 2 Quarter 3 = 10,000 + (3,000 × 7) = 31,000 − 1,000 = 30,000 units

Year 2 Quarter 4 = 10,000 + (3,000 × 8) = 34,000 − 2,000 = 32,000 units

35 (a)

Year	Actual Overheads	Cost index	Adjustment factor	Costs at 20Y1 price level
	£			£
20X8	143,040	192	× 235/192	175,075
20X9	156,000	200	× 235/200	183,300
20Y0	152,320	224	× 235/224	159,800
20Y1	172,000	235	× 235/235	172,000

(b) If the forecast number of machine hours is 3,100 and the cost index is 250:

Forecast overhead costs = [£33,000 + (£47 × 3,100 hours)] × (250/235)

= £178,700 × (250/235)

= £190,106

36 C = F + Vx

14,520 = 7,788 + V(3,300)

6,732 = 3,300V

V = 2.04

PREPARING CASH BUDGETS

CASH RECEIPTS

37 (i)

	April £	May £	June £
Sales	20,000	20,400	20,808
Cash receipts (40%)	8,000	8,160	8,323
Credit sales (60%)	12,000	12,240	12,485
Receipts from receivables (30%)		3,600	3,672
(65%)			7,800
Total cash receipts for June			19,795

(ii)

	£
Opening receivables	0
Total credit sales	36,725
Total receipts from receivables	−15,072
Closing receivables	21,653

Note: Total sales (£61,208) and total receipts (£39,555) can be used instead of total credit sales and total receipts from receivables instead to get the same answer.

(iii) £12,240 × 5% = £612

38

	June	July	August	September
Sales (units)		5,000	4,000	4,400
£ per unit		60	65	65
Total sales		300,000	260,000	286,000
Credit sales (sales units − 2,500 units) × £ per unit	103,500	150,000	97,500	123,500
Cash sales (2,500 units × £ per unit)		150,000	162,500	162,500
In month (credit sales × 60% × 98%)		88,200	57,330	72,618
Month following (credit sales × 40%)		41,400	60,000	39,000
Cash receipts		279,600	279,830	274,118

ANSWERS TO PRACTICE QUESTIONS : SECTION 2

39 (a)

	March £	April £	May £	June £
Monthly credit sales receipts	59,156	61,272	54,786	69,212

Workings:

	January	February	March	April	May	June
Total sales	61,000	72,000	54,000	72,500	81,600	92,000
Credit sales 92%	56,120	66,240	49,680	66,700	75,072	84,640
1 month after sale		16,836	19,872	14,904	20,010	22,522
2 months after sale			39,284	46,368	34,776	46,690
Total credit receipts			59,156	61,272	54,786	69,212

(b) The trade receivables balance at the end of June is forecast to be £137,190

Workings:

All June credit sales outstanding = 92,000 × 92%	= £84,640
70% May credit sales outstanding = 81,600 × 92% × 70%	= £52,550
Total outstanding	= £137,190

40 (a) C

March total sales × 15%	£6,600
February total sales × 85% × 60%	£31,620
January total sales × 85% × 40%	£17,340
Total	£55,560

(b) The trade receivables balance at the end of March is forecast to be £58,480

Workings:

All March credit sales outstanding = £44,000 × 85%	= £37,400
40% February credit sales outstanding = £62,000 × 85% × 40%	= £21,080
Total outstanding	= £58,480

41

	April	May
Total sales receipts £	378	391

The trade receivables balance at the end of May is forecast to be £343.

42

	April £	May £
Total sales receipts	14,175	17,985

The trade receivables balance at the end of May is forecast to be £24,140.

43

	April	May	June
Cash sales	15,000	15,000	15,000
Credit sales receipts	146,500	164,400	200,475
Total receipts	161,500	179,400	215,475

Workings:

Cash sales = 5,000 × £3 = £15,000

Credit sales:

	April £	May £	June £
Credit sales	198,000	206,250	214,500
Receipts			
February credit sales	101,500		
March credit sales	45,000	105,000	
April credit sales		59,400	138,600
May credit sales			61,875
Total credit sales receipts	146,500	164,400	200,475

44

	October	November	December
Cash sales (50%)	300,000	340,000	450,000
Credit sales receipts	300,000	300,000	340,000
Total cash received	600,000	640,000	790,000

Workings:

Total sales

September = 20,000 × £30 = £600,000

October = 15,000 × £40 = £600,000

November = 17,000 × £40 = £680,000

December = 18,000 × £50 = £900,000

Credit sales:

	September £	October £	November £	December £
Credit sales (50%)	300,000	300,000	340,000	450,000
Receipts				
September credit sales		300,000		
October credit sales			300,000	
November credit sales				340,000

ANSWERS TO PRACTICE QUESTIONS : SECTION 2

45

	July	August	September
Credit sales receipts	10,156	11,349	10,599

Workings:

	April £	May £	June £	July £	August £	September £
Credit sales	9,375	12,000	10,015	11,365	10,800	12,495

	July £	August £	September £
Receipts			
April credit sales	3,750		
May credit sales	2,400	4,800	
June credit sales	4,006	2,003	4,006
July credit sales		4,546	2,273
August credit sales			4,320
Total credit sales receipts	10,156	11,349	10,599

46

	Cash receipts	£
Month 4	£108,000 × 20%	21,600
Month 3	£120,000 × 80% × 40% × 0.985	37,824
Month 2	£105,000 × 80% × 30%	25,200
Month 1	£90,000 × 80% × 28%	20,160
	Total receipts	**104,784**

CASH PAYMENTS

47

Skilled		£
Product A	1,750 units × 2 hours/unit × £10/hour	35,000
Product B	5,000 units × 2 hours/unit × £10/hour	100,000
Unskilled		
Product A	1,750 units × 3 hours/unit × £7/hour	36,750
Product B	5,000 units × 4 hours/unit × £7/hour	140,000
		311,750

48 D

Paid hours including idle time = 2,400 × 100/80 = 3,000

Budgeted labour cost = 3,000 hours × £10 = £30,000

49

	April £	May £
Settlement of trade payable	2,320	2,000

50 (a)

	£
Opening balance	0
Purchase July to September	17,250
Payments July to September	7,800
Closing balance	9,450

(b)

	October £	November £
Purchases	5,850	6,100

Workings:

	July £	August £	September £	October £	November £	December £
Purchases	5,500	5,750	6,000	6,250	6,500	6,750
1 month after purchase		2,200	2,300	2,400	2,500	2,600
2 months after purchase			3,300	3,450	3,600	3,750

51 (a)

	April £	May £
Settlement of trade payables	14,880	9,120

Workings

		£
April:	All of January's outstanding balance	5,280
	February £8,640 ÷ 60 × 20	2,880
	March £16,800 × 40%	6,720
	Total	14,880
May:	February £8,640 ÷ 60 × 40	5,760
	March £16,800 × 20%	3,360
	Total	9,120

ANSWERS TO PRACTICE QUESTIONS : **SECTION 2**

(b)

	January £	February £	March £	April £	May £
Expenses	4,512	4,951	5,541	5,745	6,785
Total cost to be included in cash budget	23,512	23,951	24,541	4,745	5,785

Monthly depreciation = £60,000 × 20% = £12,000 ÷ 12 = £1,000

Purchase of machine = £60,000 ÷ 3 = £20,000

52

	October £000	November £000	December £000
Trade payables	120	120	120
Direct labour	210	210	560
Administration cost	60	60	60
Production costs	105	105	280
Distribution costs	21	21	56
Non-current asset purchase	300	25	–
Total payments	816	541	1,076

Workings:

	September	October	November	December
Sales units 000s	20	15	15	15
Production units 000s	15	15	15	40
Purchase value £000	15 × 8 = 120	15 × 8 = 120	15 × 8 = 120	40 × 8 = 320
Payments £000		120	120	120
Labour £000		15 × 2 × 7 = 210	15 × 2 × 7 = 210	40 × 2 × 7 = 560
Admin £000		90 – 30 = 60	90 – 30 = 60	90 – 30 = 60
Production £000		15 × (10 – 3) = 105	15 × (10 – 3) = 105	40 × (10 – 3) = 280
Distribution £000		210 × 10% = 21	210 × 10% = 21	560 × 10% = 56

53 B

	May £
Purchases	124,000 × 42% = 52,080
Wages	8,100
Expenses	12,200
New machine	39,000 ÷ 3 = 13,000
Total payments	85,380

54

	April £	May £
Supervisor	1,800	1,800
Standard hours	23,400	22,200
Overtime	2,250	2,550
Total labour costs	**27,450**	**26,550**

55

	Period 10 £	Period 11 £	Period 12 £
Current terms	304,500	308,250	312,750
Competitor terms	329,000	207,000	214,000
Option 1	400,200	270,600	290,400
Option 2	412,050	292,575	299,625

Workings:

Current terms

	10	11	12
Period of purchase	£31,500	£30,750	£33,000
Period following purchase	£150,000	£157,500	£153,750
2 periods following purchase	£123,000	£120,000	£126,000
Total	**£304,500**	**£308,250**	**£312,750**

Competitor terms

	10	11	12
Period of purchase	£126,000	£123,000	£132,000
Period following purchase	£80,000	£84,000	£82,000
2 periods following purchase	£123,000	£0	£0
Total	**£329,000**	**£207,000**	**£214,000**

Option 1

	10	11	12
Period of purchase	£277,200	£270,600	£290,400
Period following purchase	£0	£0	£0
2 periods following purchase	£123,000	£0	£0
Total	**£400,200**	**£270,600**	**£290,400**

Option 2

	10	11	12
Period of purchase	£148,050	£144,525	£155,100
Period following purchase	£141,000	£148,050	£144,525
2 periods following purchase	£123,000	£0	£0
Total	**£412,050**	**£292,575**	**£299,625**

ANSWERS TO PRACTICE QUESTIONS : SECTION 2

56

	July £000	August £000	September £000	October £000
Sales	100	90	125	140
Cost of sales (sales/125 × 100)	80	72	100	112
Opening inventory	40	36	50	56
Closing inventory*	36	50	56	
Purchase (cost of sale − opening + closing)	76	86	106	
Paid		(i) 76	(ii) 86	(iii) 106

*Closing inventory = 0.5 × Following month's cost of sales

57

	July £	August £
April collected	6,000	0
May collected	19,200 × 50 ÷ 80 = 12,000	19,200 × 30 ÷ 80 = 7,200
June	28,400 × 20% = 5,680	28,400 × 50% = 14,200
Settlement of trade payables	23,680	21,400

58

(a)

Month	July	August	September	October
Total payment	Standard 340,000 × 80% = 272,000 Overtime = 90,000 NIC = 32,000 **Total £394,000**	Standard 360,000 × 80% = 288,000 Overtime = 340,000 × 20% = 68,000 NIC Standard = 272,000 × 10% = 27,200 NIC Overtime = 90,000 × 12% = 10,800 **Total £394,000**	Standard 350,000 × 80% = 280,000 Overtime = 360,000 × 20% = 72,000 NIC Standard = 288,000 × 10% = 28,800 NIC Overtime = 68,000 × 12% = 8,160 Bonus = £125,000 **Total £513,960**	Standard 400,000 × 80% = 320,000 Overtime = 350,000 × 20% = 70,000 NIC Standard = 280,000 × 10% = 28,000 NIC Overtime = 72,000 × 12% = 8,640 NIC Bonus = 125,000 × 12% = 15,000 **Total £441,640**

(b)   400,000 × 20% × 12% = **£9,600**

CASH BUDGETS

59 (a)

	June	July	August
	£	£	£
Material usage	8,000	9,000	10,000
Less: Opening inventory	5,000	3,500	6,000
Closing inventory	3,500	6,000	4,000
Purchases	6,500	11,500	8,000

(b) Cash budgets, June – August

	June	July	August
	£	£	£
Receipts of cash			
Cash sales	4,500	5,000	6,000
Credit sales	29,500	40,500	45,000
	34,000	45,500	51,000
Cash payments			
Wages	12,000	13,000	14,500
Overheads	6,500	7,000	8,000
Direct materials	6,500	11,500	8,000
Taxation	–	25,000	–
	25,000	56,500	30,500
Surplus/(deficit) for month	9,000	(11,000)	20,500
Opening balance	11,750	20,750	9,750
Closing balance	20,750	9,750	30,250

(c) Cash budgets are an important part of business planning. They highlight future surpluses of cash (enabling managers to make appropriate plans for investing the surplus) and shortfalls of cash (enabling managers to take appropriate action in advance, perhaps by advising their bank of overdraft requirements or raising funds from other sources).

60 Cash flow forecast for the three months ended 30 September 2006

	July	Aug	Sept
	£	£	£
Receipts			
From receivables (W1)	10,250	11,125	12,237
Payments			
To payables (W2)	5,100	5,559	6,059
Packing costs	1,800	1,800	1,800
Sundry expenses	800	800	800
Total	7,700	8,159	8,659
Net cash flow	2,550	2,966	3,578
Balance brought forward	–6,000	–3,450	–484
Balance carried forward	–3,450	–484	3,094

Workings:

(W1) **Receipts from receivables**

	May	June	July	Aug	Sept
	£	£	£	£	£
Sales	10,000	10,000	11,000	12,100	13,310
Receipts					
May	2,500	6,000	1,500		
June		2,500	6,000	1,500	
July			2,750	6,600	1,650
Aug				3,025	7,260
Sept					3,327
			10,250	11,125	12,237

(W2) **Payments to payables**

€7,080 × 0.7203 = £5,099.724 rounded to the nearest £ = £5,100

	May	June	July	Aug	Sept
	£	£	£	£	£
Purchase	5,100	5,100	5,559	6,059	6,604
Paid next month			5,100	5,559	6,059

61

	June £	July £	August £
RECEIPTS			
Cash sales	1,100	1,200	2,300
Credit sales	40,810	60,540	70,990
Bank loan	0	30,000	0
Total receipts	41,910	91,740	73,290
Payments			
Purchases	−42,111	−20,804	−41,305
Wages	−18,000	−11,000	−12,100
Expenses	−2,555	−1,543	−1,100
Capital expenditure	0	0	−2,000
Bank loan repayment	0	0	−3,240
Overdraft interest	−100	−517	0
Total payments	−62,766	−33,864	−59,745
Net cash flow	−20,856	57,876	13,545
Opening bank balance	−5,000	−25,856	32,020
Closing bank balance	−25,856	32,020	45,565

62

	April £	May £	June £
RECEIPTS			
Cash sales	8,100	8,400	9,150
Credit sales	26,690	29,550	32,850
Bank loan	100,000	0	0
Total receipts	134,790	37,950	42,000
PAYMENTS			
Purchases	−15,600	−16,224	−16,873
Wages	−8,000	−8,000	−8,000
Expenses	−4,750	−4,950	−5,125
Tax payment	−60,000	0	0
Bank loan repayment	0	−5,050	−5,050
Overdraft interest	0	0	0
Total payments	−88,350	−34,224	−35,048
Net cash flow	46,440	3,726	6,952
Opening bank balance	50,000	96,440	100,166
Closing bank balance	96,440	100,166	107,118

Workings:

	April £	May £	June £
Cash sales	40,500 × 20% = 8,100	42,000 × 20% = 8,400	45,750 × 20% = 9,150

	April £	May £	June £
Credit sales:			
From February	32,500 × 50% = 16,250		
From March	34,800 × 30% = 10,440	34,800 × 50% = 17,400	
From April		40,500 × 30% = 12,150	40,500 × 50% = 20,250
From May			42,000 × 30% = 12,600
Total credit sales receipts	26,690	29,550	32,850

	February £	March £	April £	May £	June £
Credit purchases	15,000	15,000 × 1.04 = 15,600	15,600 × 1.04 = 16,224	16,224 × 1.04 = 16,873	16,873 × 1.04 = 17,548
Purchase payments		15,000	15,600	16,224	16,873

Monthly bank loan repayment = (£100,000 ÷ 20) + £50 = £5,050

63

	July £	August £	September £
RECEIPTS			
Cash sales	1,650	1,950	2,400
Credit sales	8,325	9,150	10,250
Bank loan	12,960	0	0
Interest receivable	18	0	0
Total receipts	22,953	11,100	12,650
PAYMENTS			
Purchases	−7,000	−7,210	−7,426
Wages	−4,000	−4,000	−4,000
Expenses	−1,250	−1,750	−2,000
Dividend payment	−15,000	0	0
Bank loan repayment	0	−396	−396
Overdraft interest	0	−7	−30
Total payments	−27,250	−13,363	−13,852
Net cash flow	−4,297	−2,263	−1,202
Opening bank balance	3,600	−697	−2,960
Closing bank balance	−697	−2,960	−4,162

Workings:

	July £	August £	September £
Cash sales	11,000 × 15% = 1,650	13,000 × 15% = 1,950	16,000 × 15% = 2,400

	July £	August £	September £
Credit sales:			
From May	9,000 × 40% = 3,600		
From June	10,500 × 45% = 4,725	10,500 × 40% = 4,200	
From July		11,000 × 45% = 4,950	11,000 × 40% = 4,400
From August			13,000 × 45% = 5,850
Total credit sales receipts	8,325	9,150	10,250

	June £	July £	August £	September £	October £
Credit purchases	7,000	7,000 × 1.03 = 7,210	7,210 × 1.03 = 7,426	7,426 × 1.03 = 7,649	7,649 × 1.03 = 7,879
Purchase payments		7,000	7,210	7,426	7,649

Monthly bank loan repayment = (£12,960 × 1.1) ÷ 36 = £396

64

	Month 3 £	Month 4 £
RECEIPTS		
Sales receipts	672,450	682,670
Rental income		2,600
Investment income	2,083	2,083
Sale of non-current asset	31,000	
Total receipts	705,533	687,353
PAYMENTS		
Purchases	−40,150	−50,200
Wages and salaries	−94,700	−92,100
General Expenses	−6,000	−5,000
Mortgage payment	−5,583	−5,583
VAT payment to HMRC	−34,000	
Purchase of non-current assets	−£4,950	−£4,950
Overdraft interest		
Total payments	−185,383	−157,833
Net cash flow	520,150	529520
Opening bank balance	160,000	680,150
Closing bank balance	680,150	1,209,670

ANSWERS TO PRACTICE QUESTIONS : SECTION 2

Workings:

	Month 3 £	Month 4 £
Rental income		£31,200 ÷ 12 = £2,600
Investment income	(£500,000 × 5%) ÷ 12 = £2,083	(£500,000 × 5%) ÷ 12 = £2,083
Sale of non-current asset	(£48,000 × 50%) + £7,000 = £31,000	
Mortgage payment	(£750,000 × 80%) ÷ 15 ÷ 12 = £3,333 (£750,000 × 80%) × 0.045 ÷ 12 = £2,250 Total = £5,583	(£750,000 × 80%) ÷ 15 ÷ 12 = £3,333 (£750,000 × 80%) × 0.045 ÷ 12 = £2,250 Total = £5,583
VAT payment to HMRC	VAT on sales = £510,100 × 20% = £102,020 VAT on purchases = £340,100 × 20% = £68,020 VAT payment = £102,020 – £68,020 = £34,000	
Purchase of non-current assets	(£54,000 × 55%) ÷ 6 = –£4,950	(£54,000 × 55%) ÷ 6 = –£4,950

65

Cash budget	Period 5 £	Period 6 £
Receipts		
Receipts from sales	100,500	106,250
Insurance claim		125,000 × 90% × 20% = £22,500
Dividend receipt	50,000 ÷ 1.22 = £40,984	
Receipt from sale of statue	10,000 ÷ 80 × 100 = £12,500	
Total receipts	100,500 + 40,984 + 12,500 = £153,984	106,250 + 22,500 = £128,750
Payments		
Purchases	(8,510)	(9,400)
Payroll payments to employees	80,300 × 88% = (£70,664)	80,500 × 88% = (£70,840)
Payments to HMRC	80,000 × 12% + 16,000 = (£25,600)	80,300 × 12% + 16,060 = (£25,696)
Recruitment cost of the CEO	7,000 + 150,000 × 20% = (£37,000)	
Other expenses	(12,050)	(16,507)
Total payments	8,510 + 70,664 + 25,600 + 37,000 + 12,050 = (£153,824)	9,400 + 70,840 + 25,696 + 16,507 = (£122,443)
Net cash flow	153,984 – 153,824 = £160	128,750 – 122,443 = £6,307
Opening bank balance	8,250	£8,410
Closing bank balance	8,250 + 160 = £8,410	8,410 + 6,307 = £14,717

ANALYSING AND MONITORING CASH BUDGETS

SENSITIVITY ANALYSIS

66 Offering prompt payment discounts to customers should **decrease** the time taken to recover debts. However, it will also **reduce** the total cash received.

This should **increase** liquidity but **reduce** the overall profitability.

67 Taking advantage of early settlement discounts offered by suppliers will **reduce** the amount we pay overall but having to pay **earlier** may mean there is a **bigger** strain on our cash flows.

68 (a)

	Period 1 (£)	Period 2 (£)	Period 3 (£)	Period 4 (£)	Period 5 (£)
Original value of forecast sales	90,000	95,000	102,500	94,500	107,500
Original timing of receipts			97,250	100,100	98,400
Revised value of forecast sales	72,000	76,000	82,000	75,600	86,000
Revised timing of receipts			75,000	78,960	79,200

Workings:

Original timing of receipts:

Period 3 = (£95,000 × 70%) + (£102,500 × 30%) = £97,250

Period 4 = (£102,500 × 70%) + (£94,500 × 30%) = £100,100

Period 5 = (£94,500 × 70%) + (£107,500 × 30%) = £98,400

Revised value of forecast receipts:

Period 1 = £90,000 × 80% = £72,000

Period 2 = £95,000 × 80% = £76,000

Period 3 = £102,500 × 80% = £82,000

Period 4 = £94,500 × 80% = £75,600

Period 5 = £107,500 × 80% = £86,000

Revised timing of receipts:

Period 3 = (£82,000 × 10%) + (£76,000 × 50%) + (£72,000 × 40%) = £75,000

Period 4 = (£75,600 × 10%) + (£82,000 × 50%) + (£76,000 × 40%) = £78,960

Period 5 = (£86,000 × 10%) + (£75,600 × 50%) + (£82,000 × 40%) = £79,200

(b)

	Period 3 (£)	Period 4 (£)	Period 5 (£)
Original timing of payments	22,354	28,601	21,660
Revised timing of payments	21,431	23,603	27,213

Workings:

Revised timing of payments

Period 3 = (£22,354 × 20%) + (£21,200 × 80%) = £21,431

Period 4 = (£28,601 × 20%) + (£22,354 × 80%) = £23,603

Period 5 = (£21,600 × 20%) + (£28,601 × 80%) = £27,213

(c)

	Period 3 (£)	Period 4 (£)	Period 5 (£)
Original net cash flow	5,632	5,162	5,893
Changes in sales receipts	−22,250	−21,140	−19,200
Changes in purchase payments	923	4,998	−5,553
Revised net cash flow	−15,695	−10,980	−18,860
Opening bank balance	8,597	−7,098	−18,078
Closing bank balance	−7,098	−18,078	−36,938

69 (a)

	Period 1 (£)	Period 2 (£)	Period 3 (£)	Period 4 (£)	Period 5 (£)
Original value of forecast sales	120,000	135,000	97,500	133,500	112,500
Original timing of receipts			127,500	104,700	129,300
Revised value of forecast sales	84,000	94,500	68,250	93,450	78,750
Revised timing of receipts			87,150	78,540	85,470

Workings:

Original timing of receipts:

Period 3 = (£135,000 × 80%) + (£97,500 × 20%) = £127,500

Period 4 = (£97,500 × 80%) + (£133,500 × 20%) = £104,700

Period 5 = (£133,500 × 80%) + (£112,500 × 20%) = £129,300

Revised value of forecast receipts:

Period 1 = £120,000 × 70% = £84,000

Period 2 = £135,000 × 70% = £94,500

Period 3 = £97,500 × 70% = £68,250

Period 4 = £133,500 × 70% = £93,450

Period 5 = £112,500 × 70% = £78,750

Revised timing of receipts:

Period 3 = (£84,000 × 20%) + (£94,500 × 60%) + (£68,250 × 20%) = £87,150

Period 4 = (£94,500 × 20%) + (£68,250 × 60%) + (£93,450 × 20%) = £78,540

Period 5 = (£68,250 × 20%) + (£93,450 × 60%) + (£78,750 × 20%) = £85,470

(b)

	Period 3 (£)	Period 4 (£)	Period 5 (£)
Original timing of payments	58,500	80,100	67,500
Revised timing of payments (Working)	47,250	50,022	50,778

Workings:

	Period 1	Period 2	Period 3	Period 4	Period 5
Revised sales volume (70%) (items)		630	455	623	525
Revised purchases (× 90) (£)	56,700	40,950	56,070	47,250	
60% paid one month later (£)		34,020	24,570	33,642	28,350
40% two months later (£)			22,680	16,380	22,428
Revised payments (£)			47,250	50,022	50,778

(c)

	Period 3 (£)	Period 4 (£)	Period 5 (£)
Original net cash flow	52,362	51,986	53,695
Changes in sales receipts	–40,350	–26,160	–43,830
Changes in purchase payments	11,250	30,078	16,722
Revised net cash flow	23,262	55,904	26,587
Opening bank balance	18,597	41,859	97,763
Closing bank balance	41,859	97,763	124,350

70 (a)

	Period 1 (£)	Period 2 (£)	Period 3 (£)	Period 4 (£)	Period 5 (£)
Period 1 sales	55,860	28,500	9,500		
Period 2 sales		61,446	31,350	10,450	
Period 3 sales			58,653	29,925	9,975
Period 4 sales				89,376	45,600
Period 5 sales					97,755
Revised forecast sales receipts	55,860	89,946	99,503	129,751	153,330

Workings:

	Period 1	Period 2	Period 3	Period 4	Period 5
Period 1 sales	95,000 × 60% × 98%	95,000 × 30	95,000 × 10%		
Period 2 sales		104,500 × 60% × 98%	104,500 × 30%	104,500 × 10%	
Period 3 sales			99,750 × 60% × 98%	99,750 × 30%	99,750 × 10%
Period 4 sales				152,000 × 60% × 98%	152,000 × 30%
Period 5 sales					166,250 × 60% × 98%

(b) Total receipts from sales in periods 1 to 3 **increase** by **6.9%** if the settlement discount is offered.

Workings:

Original receipts in periods 1 to 3 = £28,500 + £97,850 + £103,075 = £229,425

Revised receipts in periods 1 to 3 = £55,860 + £89,946 + £99,503 = £245,309

Difference = £245,309 − £229,425 = £15,884

Difference as a percentage of original = £15,884 ÷ 229,425 × 100 = 6.9%

71 (a)

	Period 1 (£)	Period 2 (£)	Period 3 (£)	Period 4 (£)	Period 5 (£)
Original value of forecast sales	32,400	34,200	36,900	34,020	38,700
Revised value of forecast sales	23,400	34,200	32,400	34,020	38,700
Original timing of receipts			34,425	34,812	36,810
Revised timing of receipts			29,250	33,687	35,010

Workings:

Revised value of forecast sales:

Period 1 = £32,400 − (500 × £18) = £23,400

Period 3 = £36,900 − (250 × £18) = £32,400

Revised timing of receipts:

Period 3 = (£32,400 × 35%) + (£34,200 × 25%) + (£23,400 × 40%) = £29,250

Period 4 = (£34,020 × 35%) + (£32,400 × 25%) + (£34,200 × 40%) = £33,687

Period 5 = (£38,700 × 35%) + (£34,020 × 25%) + (£32,400 × 40%) = £35,010

(b)

	Period 3 (£)	Period 4 (£)	Period 5 (£)
Payments for purchases	18,650	18,315	19,810

Workings:

	Period 1	Period 2	Period 3	Period 4	Period 5
Sales volume	1,300	1,900	1,800	1,890	2,150
Purchases £	19,000	18,000	18,900	21,500	
Payments					
From Period 1		19,000 × 35%	19,000 × 65%		
From Period 2			18,000 × 35%	18,000 × 65%	
From Period 3				18,900 × 35%	18,900 × 65%
From Period 4					21,500 × 35%
Total payments			18,650	18,315	19,810

(c)

	(£)
Opening bank balance period 3	3,200
Total sales receipts	97,947
Total purchase payments	−56,775
Closing bank balance period 5	44,372

72 (a)

	Period 1 (£)	Period 2 (£)	Period 3 (£)	Period 4 (£)	Period 5 (£)
Revised value of forecast sales	26,307	26,919	28,515	27,651	29,366
Revised timing of receipts			26,883	27,667	28,297

Workings:

	Period 1	Period 2	Period 3	Period 4	Period 5
Sales value (£)	30,100	30,800	32,620	31,640	33,600
Sales volume (value ÷ £14)	2,150	2,200	2,330	2,260	2,400
Revised sales volume (92%)	1,978	2,024	2,144	2,079	2,208
Revised sales value (£13.30)	26,307	26,919	28,515	27,651	29,366
Revised timing of receipts					
From Period 1	26,307 × 15%	26,307 × 40%	26,307 × 45%		
From Period 2		26,919 × 15%	26,919 × 40%	26,919 × 45%	
From Period 3			28,515 × 15%	28,515 × 40%	28,515 × 45%
From Period 4				27,651 × 15%	27,651 × 40%
From Period 5					29,366 × 15%
Total receipts			26,883	27,667	28,297

(b)

	Period 3 (£)	Period 4 (£)	Period 5 (£)
Revised timing of payments	7,500	8,493	9,656

ANSWERS TO PRACTICE QUESTIONS : SECTION 2

Workings:

	Period 3 (£)	Period 4 (£)	Period 5 (£)
From Period 1	8,580 × 30%		
From Period 2	7,600 × 30%	7,600 × 30%	
From Period 3	6,820 × 40% × 97%	6,820 × 30%	6,820 × 30%
From Period 4		10,740 × 40% × 97%	10,740 × 30%
From Period 5			11,310 × 40% × 97%
Total payments	7,500	8,493	9,656

(c)

	Period 3 (£)	Period 4 (£)	Period 5 (£)
Original net cash flow	276	153	219
Changes in sales receipts	−4,827	−4,463	−4,323
Changes in purchase payments	100	−1,673	1,084
Revised net cash flow	−4,451	−5,983	−3,020
Opening bank balance	790	−3,661	−9,644
Closing bank balance	−3,661	−9,644	−12,664

73 (a)

	Period 1 (£)	Period 2 (£)	Period 3 (£)
Payments			
Purchases	14,400	16,800	18,144
Other production expenses	6,420	6,634	7,169
Wages and salaries	8,250	9,020	9,225
Rent	12,000	12,400	12,400
Total payments	41,070	44,854	46,938

Workings:

	Period 1 (£)	Period 2 (£)	Period 3 (£)
Payments			
Purchases	15,000 × 96%	17,500 × 96%	18,900 × 96%
Other production expenses	6,000 × 1.07	6,200 × 1.07	6,700 × 1.07
Wages and salaries	8,250	8,800 × 1.025	9,000 × 1.025
Rent	12,000	12,000 + 400	12,000 + 400

(b) The effect of the changes to payments is to **increase** the quarterly cash outflow by **£712**.

Workings:

Original total payments = £41,250 + £44,400 + £46,500 = £132,150

Revised total payments = £41,070 + £44,854 + £46,938 = £132,862

Difference = £132,862 − £132,150 = £712

74 (a)

	January (£)	February (£)	March (£)	Total (£)
Sales receipts	29,040	23,232	33,880	86,152
Payments				
Material	6,600	5,280	7,700	19,580
Labour	4,620	3,696	5,390	13,706
Overheads	6,960	6,168	7,620	20,748

Workings:

	January	February	March
Sales receipts	30,000 × 1.1 × 0.88	24,000 × 1.1 × 0.88	35,000 × 1.1 × 0.88
Payments			
Revised production	30,000 ÷ £20 × 0.88 = 1,320	24,000 ÷ £20 × 0.88 = 1,056	35,000 ÷ £20 × 0.88 = 1,540
Material	1,320 × £5	1,056 × £5	1,540 × £5
Labour	1,320 × 0.25 × £14	1,056 × 0.25 × £14	1,540 × 0.25 × £14
Overheads	£3,000 + (1,320 × £3)	£3,000 + (1,056 × £3)	£3,000 + (1,540 × £3)

(b)

	£
Original closing cash balance at 31 March	32,450
Change in sales receipts	−2,848
Change in material cost	2,670
Change in labour cost	12,994
Change in overhead cost	1,602
Revised closing cash balance at 31 March	46,868

The cumulative cash flow for periods 1 – 3 will **increase** by £14,418

Workings:

Original closing balance at 31st March = £14,750 + £89,000 − £71,300 = £32,450

75

Period	1 (£)	2 (£)	3 (£)
New machinery	−750,000	−750,000	0
Increase in sales	500,000	500,000	500,000
Receipt of cash	250,000	500,000	500,000
Net cash flow	−500,000	−250,000	500,000

The cumulative cash flow for periods 1 – 3 will **decrease** by £250,000

76 Increase in hours worked = 50 employees × 37 hours × 4 weeks × 25% = 1,850 hours

Overtime payment = 1,850 hours × £10.50 = £19,425

Increase in cash receipts = £25,000

The cumulative cash flow for the next four weeks will **increase** by £5,575

ANSWERS TO PRACTICE QUESTIONS : SECTION 2

77 (a)

Month	January £	February £	March £	April £
Revised purchases	230,000 + 290,000 + 230,000 + 270,000 = 1,025,000 1,020,000 ÷ 4 = £255,000	£255,000	£255,000	£255,000
Forecast purchase payments	255,000 × 98% × 50% = £124,950	255,000 × 98% × 50% = £124,950 255,000 × 10% = £25,500 Total £150,450	255,000 × 98% × 50% = £124,950 255,000 × 50% = £127,500 Total £252,450	255,000 × 98% × 50% = £124,950 255,000 × 50% = £127,500 Total £252,450

(b) £255,000 × 50% × 2% × 4 = **£10,200**

MONITORING CASH BUDGETS

78 (a)

	Variance £	Adverse/ Favourable
Budgeted closing bank balance	3,198	
Shortfall in receipts from receivables	6,820	A
Increase in cash sales	954	F
Decrease in payments to payables	11,566	F
Increase in cash purchases	200	A
Increase in capital expenditure	24,500	A
Decrease in wages and salaries	2,090	F
Decrease in general expenses	1,500	F
Actual closing bank balance	(12,212)	

(b) C

Delayed capital expenditure

Note: Although the other options could have resulted in a lower overdraft they are not sufficient in themselves to reduce the deficit by £12,212

(c)

Cause	Action
Rates of income tax have increased labour costs	Reduce hours worked
Customers are buying lower value products	Actively market more expensive product lines
Suppliers are insisting on earlier payments	Negotiate early settlement discount
Customers are taking more days to settle their debts	Improve credit control
Prices of raw materials have increased	Change suppliers

79

Variance	(a) Could be caused by:	(b) Corrective action:
Shortfall in receipts	Customers are taking more time to settle their debts. Decrease in sales volume/value. Inaccurate forecasting. Economic/environmental factors affecting sales.	Improve credit control. Improve product. Increase marketing/advertising. Revise future budgets.
Shortfall in cash sales	Fewer cash sales. More customers taking credit.	As above and also check that strict controls are being followed when offering credit.
Increase in payments to payables	Buying better quality raw material.	Check to see if better quality material is improving product. Arrange better payment terms.
Increase in cash purchases	Obtained discounts by buying more for cash. Some suppliers not offering credit terms.	Adjust future forecasts for cash payments. Investigate why credit terms not being offered.
Increase in capital expenditure	Earlier expenditure has been deferred. Unexpected expenditure incurred.	Better forecasting.
Decrease in wages and salaries	Training has reduced hours worked. Sales volumes declining so manufacturing is decreasing. Less overtime than budgeted. Reduction in staff numbers.	Adjust future budgets to reflect the improvements if due to efficiencies.

ANSWERS TO PRACTICE QUESTIONS : SECTION 2

80

	Budgeted (£)	Actual (£)	Variance (£)	A/F
RECEIPTS				
Cash sales	4,200	3,800	400	A
Credit sales	42,100	48,000	5,900	F
Total receipts	46,300	51,800	5,500	F
PAYMENTS				
Cash purchases	500	–1,200	700	A
Credit purchases	28,000	–35,100	7,100	A
Labour costs	2,500	–3,200	700	A
Capital expenditure	8,000	–6,000	2,000	F
General expenses	4,000	–3,800	200	F
Total payments	43,000	–49,300	6,300	A
Net cash flow	3,300	2,500	800	A

81 (a)

	£	Adverse or Favourable
Budgeted closing bank balance	6,455	
Receipts from receivables	4,756	A
Cash sales	570	A
Payments to payables	2,173	A
Cash payments	940	A
Capital expenditure	12,000	A
Wages and salaries	3,600	F
General expenses	4,136	F
Actual closing bank balance	(6,248)	

(b) Shortfall in receipts and cash sales – improve credit control, improve the product, increase advertising and marketing.

Increase in cash and credit payments – arrange better credit terms with suppliers, investigate other suppliers or materials that may be cheaper.

Capital expenditure could be delayed or another form of finance could be used.

82 **Sales (6% adverse)**

Possible reasons

- Delays in collection of cash from receivables
- Decrease in production volume therefore sales volume due to the machine breaking down
- Reduction in selling price in line with competition
- Inaccurate forecasting

Possible actions

- Improve credit control/tighten up credit terms
- Consider keeping more inventory of the product in case of emergencies (machine breaking down)
- Improvement to the product to increase sales
- Better advertising of product
- Reflect any price changes in future budgets if they are to be maintained

Investment income (18% adverse)

Possible reasons

- Drop in bank base rate which has affected the rate of interest of the investment
- Inaccurate forecasting

Possible actions

- Research other investments for a better more stable return – possibly look for a fixed interest investment
- Amend future budgets to reflect the change in interest rate.

Labour cost (9% favourable)

Possible reasons

- If production volume has dropped due to the machine breakdown direct wages may fall
- Less overtime being worked
- Reduction in staff numbers

Possible actions

- Future budgets may need to be adjusted if a reduction in manufacturing/staff numbers is to be maintained.
- If efficiencies have improved in the work force this should be reflected in future budgets.

Capital expenditure (28% adverse)

Possible reasons

- Replacement of broken machine
- Deferral of earlier planned expenditure
- Unexpected expenditure
- Price increase since budget
- Higher specification of assets purchased

Possible actions

- Better planning in the future
- Use of other forms of finance to fund purchases (leasing, hire purchase, loan)
- Deferral to a later period

LIQUIDITY MANAGEMENT

LIQUIDITY AND WORKING CAPITAL

83 C

84 D

85 80 + 40 − 45 = 75 so the correct choice is **C**

86 The cash operating cycle will decrease by 2 days – the increase in inventory holding days increases the length of the cycle, the increase in the payment period decreases the length of the cycle – the net effect is a decrease of 2 days.

87 The cash operating cycle will increase by 7 days – the increase in the receivables period increases the length of the cycle, the decrease in inventory holding days decreases the length of the cycle – the net effect is an increase of 7 days.

88 The answer is 44.24 days.

Receivables

	£		£
B/f	68,000	Returns	2,500
Sales	250,000	Cash	252,100
		Irrecoverable debts	
		(68,000 × 0.05)	3,400
		C/f	60,000
	318,000		318,000

Receivable days = 60/247.5 × (365/2) = 44.24 days

89 B

	£
Balance b/fwd	22,000
Credit sales	290,510
	312,510
Less: Balance c/fwd (£290,510 × 49/365)	(39,000)
Receipts	273,510

90 97.3 days

		Days
Inventory	(0.8/3) × 365	97.3
Trade receivables	(0.4/4) × 365	36.5
Trade payables	(0.3/3) × 365	(36.5)
Working capital cycle		97.3

91 (a)

	Working	31 May 20X5
Sales revenue	Receivable days = Rec ÷ Rev × 365 44.1 = 290,000 ÷ Rev × 365 Rev = 290,000 ÷ 44.1 × 365	2,400,000
Cost of sales	2,400,000 – 1,000,000	1,400,000
Inventories level in the statement of financial position	Inventory days = Inv ÷ COS × 365 93.9 = Inv ÷ 1,400,000 × 365 Inv = 93.9 ÷ 365 × 1,400,000	360,000
Trade payables payment period in days (1 decimal place)	190,000 ÷ 1,400,000 × 365	49.6

(b) The working capital (cash operating) cycle for DX is 44.1 + 93.9 – 49.6 = 88.4 days

92

(i)	Inventory days		220/1800 × 365	44.6
(ii)	Receivables days		350/(0.85 × 2,600) × 365	57.8
(iii)	Payables days		260/1800 × 365	52.7

93

(a) The inventory holding period is 150 ÷ 1,300 × 365 = 42 days

The trade receivables collection period is 300 ÷ 2,700 × 365 = 41 days

The trade payable payment period is 230 ÷ 1,300 × 365 = 65 days

(b) The working capital cycle is 42 + 41 – 65 = 18 days

(c) The interest cover is 550/75 = 7.3 times

(d) The quick ratio is (300 + 25)/(230 + 90) = 1.0

(e) The return on capital employed is 550/(1,400 + 2,100) = 15.7%

(f) The return on shareholders' funds is 380/2,100 = 18.1%

ANSWERS TO PRACTICE QUESTIONS : SECTION 2

94 C

Average receivables = (£10 million + £12 million)/2 = £11 million

Average trade-related receivables = 90% × £11 million = £9.9 million

Annual sales on credit = £95 million

Average collection period = (£9.9 million/£95 million) × 365 days = 38 days

95 To improve the working capital cycle, a business could **decrease** its debt collection period and/or **extend** the credit period it obtains from its suppliers.

96 The answer is £4,800.

	Current assets	Current liabilities
	£	£
Credit purchase:		
Inventory	+ 18,000	
Trade payables		+ 18,000
Credit sale:		
Trade receivables	+ 24,000	
Inventory (24,000 × 100/125)	− 19,200	

Working capital will increase by £4,800, as a result of the credit sale.

97 The answer is £6.75m

CoS = £30m × 70% = £21m

Inventory months = Inventory value/CoS × 12

2.5 = Inv/21 × 12

2.5/12 × 21 = 4.375

Receivable months = Receivables/Revenue × 12

2.0 = Receivables/30 × 12

2.0/12 × 30 = 5

Payable months = Payables/CoS × 12

1.5 = Pay/21 × 12

1.5/12 × 21 = 2.625

Working capital = £4.375 + £5 − £2.625 = £6.75m

98 Over capitalisation is a situation where a firm has **more** working capital than it needs. This often results in a business having a significant cash **surplus**.

99 (i) Overtrading means a company it growing too quickly without the long term finance to support its growth. This will result in rapid increase in turnover, high levels of inventory, receivables, payables, little increase in share capital and long term loans and problems with liquidity (large decline in cash levels) when short term funding is used to support the growth.

(ii) The actions HL could take to correct the problem could be:

- Inject more long term capital into the business by issuing more share capital or raising long term loans
- Cut back on trading and be more selective of who they sell to
- Reduce the working capital cycle to improve liquidity, i.e. chase receivables to collect cash faster, reduce inventory levels and delay payables within reason.

RAISING FINANCE

INTEREST RATES

100 A

101 B

102 D

103 B

104 A flat rate loan charges a flat rate of interest on the full amount of a loan, even after repayments are made. For example a £1,000 loan with a flat rate of 5% will charge interest of £1,000 × 5% = £50 per annum every year until maturity, even if some of the capital is repaid.

With an APR loan the interest is based on a percentage of the amount outstanding. Therefore if some of the loan amount is repaid then the interest charges reduce (as will now be based on the lower outstanding balance). APR is often term used to describe the effective rate of interest that a borrower will pay on a loan.

FINANCING OPTIONS

105 E

106 C

107 Total repayments = £5,500 × 12 = £66,000

Interest paid = £66,000 − £60,000 = £6,000

Interest rate = £6,000 ÷ £60,000 × 100 = 10%

ANSWERS TO PRACTICE QUESTIONS : SECTION 2

108 Total repayments = £4,000 × 12 × 5 = £240,000

Interest paid = £240,000 − £200,000 = £40,000

Interest rate = £40,000 ÷ £200,000 × 100 ÷ 5 years = 4%

109 100,000 × 2% = £2,000 interest pa

£2,000 × 3 = £6,000

(£100,000 + £6,000) ÷ 36 = £2,944

110

	Month 3	Month 4	Month 5	Month 6	Month 7
Forecast net cash flow	7,500	−7,500	15,000	−15,000	−10,000
Opening balance	−5,000	2,500	−5,062.50	9,937.50	−5,125.78
Closing balance before interest	2,500	−5,000	9,937.50	−5,062.50	−15,125.78
Overdraft interest to be charged	0	−62.5	0	−63.28	−189.07

111 12/250 × 100 = 4.8%

112 A

113

Statement	True	False
A floating charge is security on a loan supplied by a group of assets	✓	
A fixed charge is security on a loan supplied by a specific asset	✓	
Gearing is calculated as total debt / (total debt + equity), where total debt = long and short term debt.		✓
Higher gearing indicates greater risk to lenders and investors	✓	
Lower interest cover is less risky		✓

In CSFT, gearing is calculated as total debt / (total debt + equity). Total debt is all non-current (long term) debt ONLY.

114 (i) A Gearing = total debt / (total debt + equity) = (50,000) / (50,000 + 125,000 + 15,000) = 26.3%

(ii) B Gearing = total debt / (total debt + equity) = 1,200,000 / (1,200,000 + 2,000,000) = 37.5%.
Remember total debt is only long term debt (not overdrafts).

115 A bank loan is often **less** expensive than an overdraft, mainly due to the **lower** interest rates.

An overdraft can be **cheaper** overall because we only borrow what's needed, on a daily basis.

KAPLAN PUBLISHING

116

		Loan interest £	Capital repayments £	Arrangement fee £	Overdraft interest £	Total cost £
Option 1	Year 1	6,000	25,000	1,500	2,400	
	Year 2	4,000	25,000	–	–	
		10,000	50,000	1,500	2,400	63,900
Option 2	Year 1	6,660	37,000	1,110	–	
	Year 2	4,440	37,000	–	–	
		11,100	74,000	1,110	–	86,210

Option 1

Option 2 has the higher total cost over the two years considered.

117 Currently the company is incurring two costs that could be saved if they accepted the without recourse facility offered by Cashrich Credit plc.

Savings

Admin costs of sales ledger	£15,000
Interest – 8% of £500,000 × 85%	£34,000
Total savings	£49,000

Costs

Charges £3,000,000 × 2½%	£75,000

As the costs exceed the savings, it would not be in the company's interest to accept the facility.

118

Statement	True	False
Invoice discounting passes control of the sales ledger and credit control function to the invoice discounting company		✓

119 Hire purchase agreement

- A hire purchase agreement will enable the company to purchase the plant and pay for it in instalments over 5 years.

- Interest will be charged based on the balance outstanding and an interest rate set at the beginning of the finance term.

- The plant will remain the property of the hire purchase company until all the instalments have been made however the company will be responsible for repairs and maintenance during the term of the hire purchase agreement.

- As the company will have substantially all of the risks and rewards of ownership the plant will be shown on the statement of financial position as an asset at its full purchase price.

- The balance of the hire purchase outstanding will be shown as a liability on the statement of financial position. The amount due within one year will be included with current liabilities and the balance with non-current liabilities.

- Interest paid on the loan will be debited to the statement of profit or loss.

- The balance of the loan in non-current liabilities is classed as long term debt and will therefore be included in the gearing calculation.

- The gearing of the company will increase which could affect the company's ability to raise additional finance. The plant will not be available for other lenders to take as security because the hire purchase company will hold title until the final repayment has been made.

Lease

- This is a straight forward lease agreement where the company would hire or rent the plant, and in many ways is very similar to a hire purchase agreement except ownership of the asset will not transfer to the lessee at the end of the agreement.

- The lessor would retain ownership of the asset.

- The lessee would recognise the asset within their statement of financial position as a non-current asset (at the present value of the lease payments – this will often equal the purchase cost of the asset = £400,000, plus any additional indirect costs), and then depreciated like a normal asset over the length of the lease (6 years).

- The lessee also would recognise a lease liability (PV of lease payments – often equal to the purchase price = £400,000) as a non-current liability in the statement of financial position.

- The total lease payments in excess of the lease liability (i.e. £400,000) will be interest and spread across the length of the lease. This interest is expensed as finance costs.

- The payments will be spread over the term of the lease so cash outflows will be spread over 6 years for a 6 year lease.

- The company will show reduced profits due to the depreciation of the asset and the finance costs charged to the statement of profit or loss.

- The gearing of the company will be increased due to the lease liability which will be included as debt.

Equity injection

- The company will raise funds from the existing shareholders of the business, from new shareholders or from a combination of both.

- The additional funds raised will be used to purchase the plant outright.

- The plant will be included in non-current assets on the statement of financial position.

- There will not be any cost from this method of raising finance to the statement of profit or loss because there will be no borrowing associated with the asset and therefore no interest payments to be made.

- The equity position on the statement of financial position will increase which will have the effect of reducing gearing assuming that there is no increase in long term borrowings.

- The company will be in a stronger position to raise additional finance with lower gearing and the plant available as security.

- If the shares are offered to new investors then existing shareholders will experience a dilution of control and possibly earnings which may cause discontent.

Taking out a bank loan

- A bank loan is a contractual agreement for a specific sum, loaned for a fixed period, at an agreed rate of interest.

- The term of a loan should not exceed the life of the asset being purchased and will normally be approximately the same as the asset's useful life.

- The interest on the loan will either be fixed or variable. If the interest is variable then the interest charged will depend upon market rates of interest. If the interest on the loan is fixed rate then this is often more expensive than an overdraft or a variable rate loan. You will end up paying more for the asset than it would have cost for cash.

- The bank may only be prepared to advance the money on the basis of some security given by the business. Security can be in the form of a fixed charge or a floating charge. The bank would have the right to sell this asset if the business defaults on the loan repayments.

- The bank may impose certain restrictions or covenants which will limit the freedom of action of the management of the business, for example restrictions on payment of dividends or on other forms of finance taken out by the business.

- The loan will sit as a long term liability on the statement of financial position.

- The interest and repayment charges will be put through the statement of profit or loss.

- Gearing will be increased as there is an increase in debt finance.

Funding using bonds

- Also known as loan stock or debentures. The bond is recorded as a non-current liability on the statement of financial position and any interest to be paid will be recorded on the statement of profit or loss in the finance cost.

- Loan stock commonly has a fixed rate of interest, although in recent years a number of companies have issued floating rate debentures. They are repaid at a specified date.

- Cheaper than equity.

- Defers repayment until end of life of loan.

- It is generally cheaper to raise than a new issue of equity.

- It may be cheaper to finance than equity since debenture-holders suffer less risk and may be satisfied by a lower return. However, the gearing of the company will increase so shareholders may perceive there to be a greater risk if the company is already highly financed and may therefore require a higher return. Any future financing may be affected, as future lenders will consider the level of debt already in existence.

- The existing shareholders will retain the same degree of control.

- The company may be committed to the fixed interest payments and will therefore have less flexibility than with equity.

- In the event of any default on the interest payments, the debenture-holders would have the power to appoint a receiver to run the company.

Debt factoring

- Factoring is the sale of debts to a third party (the factor) at a discount in return for prompt cash. The debts of the company are effectively sold to a factor (normally owned by a bank). The factor takes on the responsibility of collecting the debt for a fee.

- A factor can save the company the administration costs of keeping the sales ledger up to date and the costs of debt collection.

- Non-recourse factoring is a convenient way of obtaining insurance against irrecoverable debts.

- Although factors provide valuable services, companies are sometimes wary about using them. A possible problem with factoring is that the intervention of the factor between the factor's client and the receivable could endanger trading relationships and damage goodwill. Customers might prefer to deal with the business, not a factor.

- When a nonrecourse factoring service is used, the client loses control over decisions about granting credit to its customers.

- There is no impact on the gearing of the company and very little impact on the financial statements.

120 Normal lease

- A lease has to be shown on the statement of financial position by capitalising the asset and including the loan element of the lease as borrowing (non-current liability).

- The lease includes implicit interest charges which will be charged as an expense in the statement of profit or loss (as finance costs).

- The asset will be depreciated as usual over the length of the lease (or the UEL if it is less).

- The lessee may be responsible for the upkeep and maintenance of the asset, or it may remain the responsibility of the lessor. The lease payments reflect the repayment of the value of the asset and the finance charge to the lessor.

- The cash balance will not be affected by the acquisition but will be reduced by the lease payments.

- The payments will be spread over the term of the lease, aiding short term cash flow.

- The gearing of the company will increase because the asset base increases but so does the total debt (in the form of the lease liability).

- The increase in gearing could affect the company's ability to raise additional finance.

- The net assets will be unchanged at acquisition but the debt will increase.

- The statement of profit or loss will recognise both the depreciation expense and the interest element of the lease payments but not the capital repayment element.

Short term or low value item lease

- If the lease is for 12 months or less, or the lease is for an item of low value (e.g. a telephone, laptop, office chair etc.) then the lessee can elect not to follow the normal lease treatment.

- The asset is not included within non-current assets and no lease liability is recognised on the statement of financial position.

- Lease payments are an expense in the statement of profit or loss, rather like rental payments. These are spread on a straight line basis over the length of the lease

- The lessor will normally maintain the asset.

- The gearing of the company will be unaffected as the lease is 'off balance sheet'.

- The total debt on the statement of financial position will be unaffected by the lease and the asset value is also unaffected, but a competent credit risk analyst will consider the size of the lease commitment when deciding to grant additional funding or credit.

121 Option 1

£2,500 + (60 × £800) + £2,000 = £52,500

A payment of £2,500 extra

A percentage of £2,500/£50,000 × 100 = 5%

Option 2

£2,500 + (30 × £1,750) = £55,000

A payment of £5,000 extra

A percentage of £5,000/£50,000 × 100 = 10%

Based on interest rate and overall cost – **option 1** should be chosen.

122 Option 1

Set up cost = £1,500,000 × 2% = £30,000

Total interest = £1,500,000 × 8% ÷ 12 × 18 = £180,000

Total cost of loan = £1,500,000 + £180,000 + £30,000 = £1,710,000

Monthly repayments = (£1,500,000 + £180,000) ÷ 18 = £93,333

First month's payment = £93,333 + £30,000 = £123,333

Option 2

The company will be paying the £91,836 in the final month to own the asset so the cost that needs to be spread over 17 months = £1,500,000 + £152,793 – £91,836 = £1,560,957

Monthly repayments = £1,560,957 ÷ 17 = £91,821

Total cost of hire purchase = (£91,821 × 17) + £91,836 = £1,652,793

Which can also be calculated as £1,500,000 + £152,793 = £1,652,793

Option 3

The length of the lease term is not provided so for a comparison of costs:

Repayment over 18 months of £104,166 × 18 months = £1,874,988

ANSWERS TO PRACTICE QUESTIONS : SECTION 2

123 (a) How much interest and administration charge will be paid is option 1 is taken?

Total repayments = £4,444 × 90 = £399,960

Interest = £399,960 − £300,000 = £99,960

Interest and administration charge = £99,960 + £1,500 = £101,460

(b) How much interest and administration charge will be paid if option 2 is taken?

Annual interest = £300,000 × 5% = £15,000

Interest over life of the loan = £15,000 × 7.5 years = £112,500

Interest and administration charge = £112,500 + £1,000 = £113,500

(c) How much is the quarterly repayment for option 2?

Quarterly interest = £15,000 ÷ 4 = £3,750

Quarterly capital repayment = £300,000 ÷ 30 = £10,000

Total repayment = £3,750 + £10,000 = £13,750

(d) How much interest and administration fee will be paid if option 3 is taken?

Total interest = £150,000 × 11% × 7.5yrs = £123,750

Total administration = £800 × 8 payments = £6,400

Total interest and administration = £123,750 + £6,400 = £130,150

124 (a) Complete the accounting entry which would have been made on the day the loan was received.

Account	Debit	Credit	Amount £
Current bank account	✓		1,500,000
Current loan account		✓	1,500,000 ÷ 6 = £250,000
Long-term loan account		✓	£1,500,000 − £250,000 = £1,250,000

(b) Complete the missing figures. Round your answer to the nearest £000

Extract of the Trial balance	31st March 20X7	31st March 20X6
Plant and machinery	8,000	6,300
Inventories	3,000	2,500
Trade receivables	2,100	2,100
Bank current account	60	(60)
Trade payable	(5,700)	(5,100)
Other creditors	(1,900)	(1,600)
Current portion of long term loan	(250)	(250)

KAPLAN PUBLISHING

AAT: CASH AND FINANCIAL MANAGEMENT

Long term loan	Full years repayment of £250,000 Amount outstanding = £1,125,000 – £250,000 = £875,000 (£875)	6 months repayment = 250,000 ÷ 2 = 125,000 Amount outstanding = £1,250,000 - £125,000 = £1,125,000 (£1,125)
Retained profit	(4,900)	(3,300)
Share capital	(500)	(500)
Turnover	(59,700)	(57,600)
Purchases	43,600	42,700
Other operating costs	13,300	12,600
Long term loan interest	68	40
Taxation	1,200	1,200

(c) Calculate the gearing for both years. Round your answer to the nearest whole percent.

	20X7	20X6
Gearing	875/(875 + 4900 + 500) × 100 = 13.94% = **14%**	1125/(1125 + 3300 + 500) × 100 = 22.84% = **23%**

125 Option 1: Bank Loan

Cost of Loan

Total interest £1,000,000 × 6% × 2 = £120,000

Setup cost £120,000 × 12.5% = £15,000

Total cost of loan = £135,000

Monthly repayment if arrangement fee is spread over life of the loan = £1,135,000/24 = £47,292

First month if arrangement fee is not spread = (£1,120,000 ÷ 24) + £15,000 = £61,667, then monthly payments of £46,667

Advantages of Loan

- Generally loans can be tailored to suit the business e.g. period, repayment schedule and interest rates
- Generally lower interest rates than other finance options
- The repayments are fixed so good for budgeting purposes
- Payment holidays may be allowed

Disadvantages of Loan

- Interest charged on the initial loan balance so no account taken of payments made.
- Penalties for early repayment
- Security may be needed
- Covenants may be needed
- Charge may be placed on asset or asset(s)

Accounting Treatment

- The setup fee and interest for year 1 will be charged to the statement of profit or loss in year 1 and the interest for year 2 will be charged to the statement of profit or loss in year 2.
- The credit rating may suffer
- The balance of the loan will be split between current liabilities and non-current liabilities in the statement of financial position.
- Only the current liability amount will have a bearing on the liquidity ratio.
- The non-current amount of the balance outstanding on the loan will be included in the gearing calculation.
- The gearing of the company will increase which could affect the company's ability to raise additional finance.

Option 2 Debt Factoring

Costs of Debt Factoring

Will increase non-current asset levels by £1m in the statement of financial position.

Initial cost to the company £250,000 (25% 0.25/1.0)

Invoice (debt) factoring is a way of raising finance quickly by selling your trade receivables/unpaid invoices to a debt factoring company.

The factor will pay the company to take on your outstanding invoices.

Typically they would pay 85% of the invoice values immediately.

The factor manages the sales ledger and chasing of the payment.

Suppliers are aware the credit control has been outsourced.

There are two types namely recourse and non-recourse. Recourse factoring is where the company retains the risk of bad debts. Recourse factoring is cheaper. Non-recourse factoring is where the factor takes on the risk of bad debts. Non-recourse factoring is more expensive

Advantages of Invoice Factoring

- Obtain cash quickly
- Secures more cash than an overdraft based on outstanding invoices (usually 50%)
- Reduces time and cost spend on credit control/debt collection

Disadvantages of Invoice Factoring

- Fee charged for factoring
- Factor takes over sales ledger
- Damage to customer relationships
- Alerts customers that there may be cash flow problems in the business
- Factor may impose constraints on the way you do business
- Ending a factoring arrangement could be difficult

Accounting Treatment

- Factoring fees will be recorded as an expense in the statement of profit or loss.
- With non-recourse factoring any debts not collected will be borne by the factor.
- With recourse factoring any irrecoverable debts will be borne by the business and written off to the statement of profit or loss.

Option 3 Lease

Cost of Lease

Annual lease rental payments £625,000

Monthly repayment is £625,000/12 = £52,083

Total cost is £1,250,000 over the 2 years

Advantages of Lease

- Right to use the asset
- Lease may be easier to arrange than finance to purchase the asset
- May be able to cancel the lease early or extend it if required (depending on the terms of the lease)
- Stable predictable lease payments can be budgeted for more easily.

Disadvantages of Lease

- Cost of the lease may be more expensive than obtaining finance to purchase the asset
- May have restrictions on what can be done with the asset and where it can be used
- No ownership of asset
- Commitment to make payments over lease term

Accounting Treatment

- The asset would be included within non-current assets at its value of £1m, and a lease liability recognised for the same amount within the statement of financial position
- As the asset would cost £1m to buy outright, this implies that the additional cost above this of £250,000 is interest. This would be charged as finance costs to the statement of profit or loss over the 2 years of the lease
- The asset would be depreciated as normal over the length of the lease. Therefore £1m / 2 years = £500,000 depreciation expense per year
- Gearing would be increased due to the lease liability of £1m, which would be included as debt
- There will be no initial entry in current liabilities and the liquidity ratios will be unaffected. However the regular lease payments will impact cash flow.

ANSWERS TO PRACTICE QUESTIONS : SECTION 2

126

Annual sales revenue = £1,095,000	
Factoring fee £1,095,000 × 2.5%	= £27,375
Annual interest (90% × £180,000) × 12%	= £19,440
Savings in credit control costs	(£20,000)
Net cost of factoring	£26,815

127 **£750,000**

£1,250,145 × 80% = £1,000,116 is greater than the maximum allowed.

128 B

129 B

130

	True	False
Crowdfunding obtains funding from a few wealthy investors		✓
Crowdfunding is most common with start-up and smaller businesses	✓	
Crowdfunding uses technology and online platforms to attract investors	✓	
Crowdfunding is arranged with a bank		✓
Crowdfunding can also boost brand awareness and help build a customer base	✓	
Large listed businesses often use crowdfunding		✓

INVESTING SURPLUS FUNDS

131 D

If £1 million is invested for one year at 7%, the value of the investment will be £1,000,000 × 1.07 = £1,070,000 after one year.

If £1 million is invested for three months at 6.5% per year and then for nine months at 7.5% per year, this means that the interest for the first three months will be 6.5% × 3/12 = 1.625%, and the interest for the next nine months will be 7.5% × 9/12 = 5.625%. The value of the investment after one year will therefore be:

£1,000,000 × 1.01625 × 1.05625 = £1,073,414.

This is £3,414 more than the income that would be obtained by investing at 7% for the full year.

However, there is a risk that interest rates will not rise during the first three months, and KIT will not be able to invest at 7.5% for the nine months, but only at a lower rate.

132 (a) 500,000 × 3% ÷ 12 × 10 = £12,500

(b) 500,000 × 5% ÷ 12 × 7 = £14,583

133 £100 × 5.3% ÷ £105 × 100 = 5.05%

134 Interest received = (150,000 × 6%) ÷ 2 = £4,500

Interest yield = 9,000 ÷ 175,000 × 100 = 5.14%

135 Annual interest = £800,000 × 4.5% = £36,000

Interest received = £36,000 ÷ 12 × 9 = £27,000

136 Three factors that would need to be considered when deciding how to invest short term cash surpluses are:

Maturity

A short term investment will involve investing the money for a specified period of time and receiving interest and the payment of the capital at a specified future date. The maturity date of the investment should be no longer than the duration of the cash surplus. If the cash is required before the maturity of the investment and the investment is 'cashed in' early, there will be the risk of loss of interest or capital value.

Risk v Return

Risk refers to the possibility that the investment might fall in value or that there may be some doubt about the eventual payment of interest or repayment of capital. Generally a higher risk investment will offer a higher return.

Liquidity

Liquidity refers to the ease with which an investment can be 'cashed in' without any significant loss of value or interest. All short-term investments are less liquid than cash in a bank current account, but some are more liquid than others. For example, many savings accounts or deposit accounts are reasonably liquid, as a depositor can withdraw cash immediately without penalty or for the loss of only several days' interest.

137 £54,000 × 1.086^3 = £69,164.50

138 £20,000 × 1.034 = £20,680

139 £2,500 ÷ 2 × 100 = £125,000

ANSWERS TO PRACTICE QUESTIONS : SECTION 2

140 Certificates of deposit are certificates issued by **banks** that certify that an amount of money has been deposited and will be repaid at a specific date in the future. They **can** be traded on a market. They are considered to be a **low risk** investment.

Local authority short-term loans are certificates issued by **local authorities** and backed by the government. They **can** be traded on a market. They are considered to be a **low risk investment**.

Government securities are also known as **gilt-edged** securities and **can** be traded. Interest rates are **fixed** and these types of securities are considered to be **low risk** because they **are** backed by the government.

Bank deposit accounts tend to have a **lower** return than shares, as they are much **lower** risk. They tend to have **lower** interest rates than gilts and debentures as they are a **more** liquid investment.

Shares are issued by **companies** and **can** be traded. Dividends are usually **variable**. Shares are considered to be a **high risk** investment. This is because the returns from shares are **sometime volatile** and the value of the investment is **uncertain.**

141 Each £100 nominal value block gets 4% interest this is £4.00 cash.

To have received £600 interest we must have bought £600 ÷ £4 = 150 nominal value blocks

£9,000 was invested so market price = £9,000 ÷ 150 = £60

142 £800,000 ÷ £0.50 = 1,600,000 shares

£640,000 ÷ 1,600,000 = £0.40

143 £3 ÷ £30.50 × 100 = 9.84%

144 5,000 × £1.25 = £6,250

£6,250 + £700 = £7,000

£7,000 ÷ 5,000 = **£1.40**

145

	Convertible within 45 days	Investment £20,000 or below	Interest rate 3% above base	Investment does not include shares	Low or Medium Risk
Option 1	No	Yes	Yes	No	Yes
Option 2	Yes	Yes	Yes	Yes	Yes
Option 3	Yes	No	Yes	No	No
Option 4	Yes	No	No	Yes	Yes

The company should select **Option 2**.

146 The returns given are over different time periods. It is necessary to calculate a rate per annum to enable the investments to be compared:

The annual return on the treasury bills is (£5/£995) × 365/91 = 2.02%

The annual return on the bank deposit account is 2.5%.

Treasury bills are generally considered risk free as they are guaranteed by the government of the country of issue. However during the present economic recession it has become evident that investment with countries that have previously been considered financially secure are not risk free. It should be borne in mind that the treasury bills are fixed dated and although they are negotiable this would incur costs and expose the company to price movement which will reflect the change in market interest rates. Although the return is fixed, if the company holds the bills for 91 days, market interest rates may rise with the result that the return on the treasury bills may be below market rates.

The deposit account has a variable interest rate which will introduce variability in the return, although this is likely to reflect market rates. Investments in banks are generally considered very low risk however after the world banking crisis in 2008/2009 it is now conceivable for a bank to fail. This introduces another albeit small element of risk in that there is liquidation risk of the bank itself. The deposit account lacks flexibility as it requires the company to give 30 days' notice of withdrawal or accept penalty interest charges.

The choice of investment will depend on the company's attitude to risk and whether they prefer to have a fixed return. The bank deposit account currently offers a higher return but may not continue to do so in the future.

147 Treasury bills

Treasury bills reflect the credit rating of the country, so are generally low risk. The rate of interest is generally relatively low. In this case a yield of £10 would be earned over three months, which is an effective interest rate of only 1% per quarter.

Equities

The value of equities can go down as well as up. In this case, the equity index has increased for the last 14 months. However, this cannot be taken as a guarantee of future continued good performance. The equity index may fall rather than rise over the next few months.

The risk associated with a particular share depends upon the risk associated with the market in general and the risk associated with the particular company. In this case, the proposed companies are multinationals, which can result in a lower risk due to diversification. These companies pay an annual dividend but it may not be due during the investment period.

Due to the higher risk associated with equities, the yield is generally relatively high.

Bank deposit

A bank deposit is an investment in the business of the bank. However, banks are generally very secure, such that it is normally assumed that the investment will be recovered in full.

As with treasury bills, the yield is low to reflect the low risk, so carries a low rate of interest. However, in this case, the company would be required to give 30 days' notice of any withdrawals. This gives the bank more certainty and is reflected in an increased return on the deposit, in the form of an increased interest rate.

ANSWERS TO PRACTICE QUESTIONS : SECTION 2

148

	Suitable options
A partnership has £50,000 to invest	Options 1, 2 and 3
An investing organisation requires a low risk investment	Options 2 and 4
A guaranteed interest rate of 3% is required	Options 3 and 4
The notice period needs to be less than 50 days	Options 2, 3 and 4
The investment should not include shares	Options 2 and 4

149 Land

- Historically land is deemed to be a fairly safe investment as there is a finite supply.

- However in the last decade land values have been volatile sometimes resulting in a capital loss for investors therefore it is now considered a high risk investment as the return is unknown.

- The initial investment of £250,000 may not be fully realised if the market value is lower than £250,000 at the date of sale.

- If the plan is to build on the land the planning permission will need to be sort. This will incur extra costs (e.g. legal, planning fees, advertising etc).

- Planning permission could be refused. This could have a negative impact on the value of the land. If planning permission is granted it could greatly increase the value of the land. It is unlikely that the return could be forecast with any certainty at the time of purchase.

- Land is usually seen as a long term investment and may take longer than three years to make a suitable return for the company.

- The investment can only be realised once the land is sold and the speed of this will depend upon the economic environment at the time of sale.

- The liquidity of the company may be adversely affected if they are unable to realise the full £250,000 at the end of three years.

Long term bank deposit account

- Investment in a bank deposit account is generally perceived to be a low risk option as the interest rate is fixed and a return is guaranteed.

- The return is likely to reflect the low risk and therefore be substantially less than could be earned on other investments. The initial investment is guaranteed.

- Traditionally bank deposit accounts were seen as risk free from the perspective of the loss of capital value. However in light of the global financial crisis there is a risk of loss of capital value if the deposit is not covered by a government backed guarantee scheme.

- The deposit account may have a minimum notice period to avoid early withdrawal however the funds could be available immediately, for a fee, if required even though the company would achieve a lower return than expected.

AAT: CASH AND FINANCIAL MANAGEMENT

Shares in public companies

- Shares in public companies are generally perceived to be high risk because of market volatility and lack of control over business decisions made by those running the company.
- However high returns can be achieved with the right portfolio of shares held for a reasonable period of time.
- The company might spread the risk by selecting a portfolio which includes both low risk and high risk companies.
- The return achievable cannot be identified with any certainty at the time of investment.
- As shares can be sold at any point after purchase it would take only a few days for the company to realise its cash as long as it is prepared to take the price offered at that point in time.
- The company could also realise its cash piecemeal as and when required.
- The fees for buying and selling will need to be offset against any dividends and increase in share price when calculating the return.

Certificates of deposit

- A certificate of deposit (CD) is issued by a bank or building society which certifies that a certain sum, usually a minimum of £50,000, has been deposited with it to be repaid on a specific date.
- The term can range from seven days to five years but is usually for six months.
- CDs are negotiable instruments; they can be bought and sold, therefore if the holder does not want to wait until the maturity date the CD can be sold in the money market.
- CDs offer a good rate of interest and are highly marketable.
- CD is that they can be liquidated at any time at the current market rate. The market in CDs is large and active therefore they are an ideal method for investing large cash surpluses.
- The holder of the CD at maturity has the right to take the deposit with interest. CDs are negotiable instruments; they can be bought and sold, therefore if the holder does not want to wait until the maturity date the CD can be sold in the money market.

Treasury bills

- Treasury bills are negotiable instruments issued by the government, with a maturity of less than one year. In practice, most treasury bills have a maturity of three months (91 days). Cash is available for 3 years so this may not be the most suitable form of investment.
- Treasury bills are used by a government to finance short term cash requirements.
- Treasury bills are issued at regular intervals when investors are invited to apply to buy bills in the new issue.
- Since treasury bills are debts of the government, they have a high credit quality, risk is low, and yields for investors are therefore also lower than for many other short term investments. Treasury bills issued by a government and denominated in the domestic currency should be risk free.
- Treasury bills are redeemable at face value. Since the bills are redeemable at par, investors pay less than face value to buy them.
- Although yields on treasury bills are relatively low, they can be attractive short term investments because of their risk free nature and their liquidity. There is a large and active secondary market in treasury bills in the UK.

150 Option 1

- Fixed rate so a return is guaranteed

- The return is 6%

- Liquidity depends on the terms of the investment. This option is a fixed term of 4 years. It may be possible to redeem the investment early if the money is required but there is a risk of incurring early redemption charges/penalties, usually a couple of months interest but the capital amount is safe.

- Traditionally bank deposit accounts were seen as risk free from the perspective of the loss of capital value. However in light of the global financial crisis there is a risk of loss of capital value if the deposit is not covered by a government backed guarantee scheme.

- It may be possible to sell the bond before maturity

Option 2

- High risk investment

- The company may not be a listed FTSE100 company so selling the shares may be difficult affect the liquidity of this investment

- Share prices may increase but equally they could fall so the return is very uncertain

- A thorough investigation will need to be carried out on the company in question to analyse profits and profile. Will dividends be paid?

- Helping this company to expand may well help the local area to improve by providing much needed employment which in turn may improve the image of the investing companies. If it fails then this may have a negative impact on the investing companies

Option 3

- Very high risk investment

- Need to investigate the report regarding the abundance of oil as if the report is false the entire investment could be lost

- As with option 2 – it may be difficult to sell the shares if this company is not a listed company affecting liquidity

- A thorough investigation, including a site visit, will need to be carried out on the company in question to analyse profits and profile

- Ethical issues/damage to reputation for any investor if the claims of child labour and poor health and safety are true

151 (a) (1,500 × 5%) + (5,000 × 8%) + (1,000 × 2.5%) + (750 × 1.2%) = 75 + 400 + 25 + 9 = 509

509 ÷ 8,250 × 100 = **6.2%**

(b) 509 – 25 = 484

8,250 – 1,000 = 7,250

484 ÷ 7250 × 100 = 6.7%

152

1 **Current account**

- The amount of interest receivable on the current account is £4,000,000 × 0.4% = £16,000 per annum.
- 5-year return = £16,000 × 5 = £80,000
- Low risk – a bank account is a very safe investment
- Low return – the interest rate is very low
- High liquidity – money can be withdrawn at any point

2 **Fixed rate account**

- The amount of interest receivable on the fixed rate account is £4,000,000 × 2.4% = £96,000 per annum.
- 5-year return £480,000
- Low risk – a bank account is a safe investment, similarly to the current account above
- Fairly high return – pays more interest than other bank accounts, and the interest is guaranteed
- High liquidity – maybe penalties for early withdrawal

3 **Deposit account**

- The amount on interest receivable on the deposit account is £4,000,000 × 1.1% = £44,000 per annum.
- 5-year return £220,000
- Low risk – a bank account is a safe investment, similarly to the current account above
- Fairly low return – but higher than a standard current account
- Medium liquidity – although 90 days' notice is required to withdraw funds, it is often possible to withdraw funds quicker, however it will incur penalty fees

4 **Treasury stock**

- The amount of interest receivable on the current account is £4,000,000 × 3% = £120,000 per annum.
- 5-year return £600,000
- Low risk – government bonds are a very safe investment as it is extremely unlikely the government will default on the debt. However if the bonds are sold prior to the redemption date in five years' times then the value of the investment may vary
- High return – the 3% interest is fairly high, and the interest rate is fixed
- High liquidity – the stock is traded on a market, so can be sold at any point to release funds. However the market price may vary, changing the market value of the stock.

ANSWERS TO PRACTICE QUESTIONS : SECTION 2

5 Certificates of deposit

- The amount on interest receivable on the current account is £4,000,000 × 4% = £160,000 per annum.
- 5-year return £800,000
- Issued by banks/building societies
- Low risk – certificates of deposit are a fairly safe investment when from a reputable bank, but are more risky than treasury stock
- High return – this investment gives the highest level of interest out of the options given
- High liquidity – similarly to treasury stock, these can be traded early to release funds if needed

153

1 Land

- Traditionally land has been a safe long term investment, however in the last decade land and property prices have been more volatile, making land a more risky option
- Land is really more suitable for a long term investment, for this company who are looking to invest for two years and may need the money early, land is not really suitable
- High potential return – in the long term land prices generally rise, giving a good return. However this is not guaranteed and land prices may fall. If planning permission can be obtained then it is likely to enhance the land's value. There is no annual income from the land unless it can be rented out
- Buying and selling of the land is likely to be a time consuming process and will incur various legal and professional fees

2 30 day notice account

- The amount on interest receivable on the account is £250,000 × 1% = £2,500 per annum.
- 2-year return £5,000
- Low risk – a bank account is a safe investment.
- Fairly low return – but higher than a standard current account
- Medium liquidity – although 30 days' notice is required to withdraw funds, it is often possible to withdraw funds quicker, however it will incur penalty fees

3 Gold bars

- Gold bars are often seen as a 'safe' investment in times of market and economic uncertainty. However the value of gold can fluctuate fairly significantly in a short period of time which increases the risk
- Gold does not provide any annual income, and there are likely to be insurance and storage costs each year
- The gold bars are a very liquid investment as they can be easily sold at any time

4 Treasury bonds

- The amount of interest receivable on the current account is £250,000 × 4% = £10,000 per annum.
- 2-year return £20,000
- Low risk – government bonds are a very safe investment as it is extremely unlikely the government will default on the debt. However if the bonds are sold prior to the redemption date in five years' times then the value of the investment may vary
- High return – the 4% interest is fairly high, and the interest rate is fixed
- High liquidity – the stock is traded on a market, so can be sold at any point to release funds. However the market price may vary, changing the market value of the stock.

Recommendation

The land is not suitable for a long term investment, and the gold bars are likely to be too risky. The 30 day notice account is a good option since it provides a reasonable return and the cash can be accessed easily if required. The treasury bonds are also a good option, and provide a higher return than the notice account, but do have the risk that the market value may fall when the bonds are traded before the redemption date.

154 For irredeemable bonds: Rate of return = Interest / Bond price. Here the required return is 5% (0.05) and the bond will pay interest of £3 per year (3% × £100).

Therefore 0.05 = 3 / Bond price, so bond price = 3 / 0.05 = **£60**

155 A company makes an investment of £18,000 and receives interest of £200 per month and then is repaid a total of £19,500 in a year's time.

Total interest = (12 months × £200) + £1,500 'profit' on redemption = £3,900

Interest rate = Interest / Investment = £3,900 / £18,000 = 0.217 = **21.7%**

… ANSWERS TO PRACTICE QUESTIONS : SECTION 2

IMPACT OF REGULATIONS AND POLICIES ON FINANCING AND INVESTMENT

GOVERNMENT POLICY AND REGULATIONS

156 (i) Quantitative easing is where the central bank (Bank of England in the UK) 'prints money' by digitally creating funds which it then uses to government bonds. This has the effect of lowering interest rates and pumping more money into the economy. This in turn makes it easier for banks to lend money to people and businesses, hopefully increasing growth and stimulating the economy.

(ii) **B**

Quantitative easing is not normally considered, as it would rapidly increase the money supply, resulting in high inflation. Instead, other measures, such as reducing interest rates could be considered. However, during the ongoing financial crisis, many countries already have very low interest rates and the threat of high inflation is not considered significant compared to the need to boost liquidity in the banking system and hence the economy.

157 Central banks try to increase the amount of lending and activity in the economy indirectly, by lowering interest rates. Lower interest rates encourage people to spend, not save.

158 (i) Fiscal policy – Tax rates and government spending (e.g. public spending and infrastructure projects)

(ii) Monetary policy – Interest rates and influencing the supply of money to the economy

159

Statement	Local economy	Global economy
Online selling, either through a business's own website or via a platform such as Ebay or Amazon Marketplace allows easy access to this economy		✓
Brand awareness amongst potential customers will likely be higher in this economy	✓	
This economy usually has the potential for faster and larger growth		✓
A business is likely to have better knowledge of customer tastes and competitors in this economy	✓	
There is likely to be increased delivery, regulatory and legal costs if expanding into this economy		✓
Investing in this economy is generally more risky for a business		✓

160 B

161 D

162

Statement	True	False
The Bribery Act covers all aspects of white collar crime		✓
Suspected money laundering of amounts under £500 do not need to be reported		✓
Companies Act required a company to disclose political donations it makes	✓	
Companies Act requires directors to consider how a company's actions impact the environment and employees as well as shareholders	✓	
Money laundering regulations only cover accountants		✓

Section 3

MOCK ASSESSMENT QUESTIONS

TASK 1 (10 marks)

(a) Identify whether the following items affect cash, profit, or both cash and profit.

(3 marks)

Item	Cash	Profit	Cash and profit
Paying weekly staff wages			
Accrual for an expected telephone bill			
Dividend payment to shareholders			

The following information has been extracted for company A:

Item	Period 5 £	Period 6 £
Electricity expense	1,200	1,350
Electricity accrual	275	380

(b) Calculate the cash paid in period 6, in relation to electricity. (1 mark)

The cash paid was £_____

MJ owns a photographic business. The following forecast information has been produced.

The Statement of profit or loss for MJ's business for the year ended December 20X5 is as follows:

	£	£
Revenue		23,560
Less: Purchases		(8,844)
Gross profit		14,716
Less: Expenses		
Wages	1,200	
Rent of darkroom	2,000	
Loss on disposal of NCA	1,760	
Printing expenses	5,000	
Camera depreciation	1,000	
		(10,960)
Operating profit		3,756

KAPLAN PUBLISHING 143

AAT: CASH AND TREASURY MANAGEMENT

Additional information

1. Photographic materials are purchased when required and therefore very little inventory is maintained.

2. The balance of trade receivables at 1 January 20X5 was £2,480 and the company expects the trade receivables at 31 December to be equivalent of 10% of total sales for the year.

(c) Forecast the net change in cash position at December 20X5. **(4 marks)**

	£
Operating profit	3,756
Change in trade receivables	
Depreciation	
Loss on disposal	
Net change in cash position	

Company P have an opening balance on its 'Land and Buildings' account of £285,000. During the year, depreciation of £25,000 was expensed and a building with a carry value of £110,000 was revalued to its fair value of £150,000. No disposals were made, and at year end 'Land and Buildings' had a balance of £475,000.

(d) How much did company P spend on additions of Land and Buildings during the year?

£ ☐ **(2 marks)**

TASK 2 (15 marks)

Yasmin is a photographer and is investigating the price of material A over the last few years.

The price for the last four years is given below.

(a) Prepare an index for the price of material A using 20X1 as the base period (to one decimal place). **(2 marks)**

Year	20X1	20X2	20X3
Price	34p	41p	45p
Index			

Yasmin uses the least squares regression line to forecast sales when she attends a wedding. The regression line has been identified as:

y = 100 + 50x

where y is the number of pictures sold and x is the number of guests in attendance.

Yasmin will be attending the wedding of Charlie and Sam who will have 350 guests in attendance.

(b) Complete the following sentence. **(1 mark)**

The forecast sales of pictures for Charlie and Sam's wedding is _____

This is a summer wedding. Yasmin always increases the sales volume by 5% for summer weddings.

(c) **Complete the following sentence.** (1 mark)

The adjusted forecast sales of pictures is _____

Yasmin buys in photographic paper at £0.12 per sheet of 6" × 4" and she wishes to achieve a 20% margin or a 40% mark up.

(d) **Calculate the forecast selling price of the product** (2 marks)

The forecast selling price to achieve a 20% margin is £_____ (to the nearest penny)

The forecast selling price to achieve a 40% mark-up is £_____ (to the nearest penny)

The cash budget for Yasmin for the three months ended March has been partially completed. The following information is to be incorporated and the cash budget completed.

- A bank loan of £5,000 has been negotiated and this will be paid into the business bank account in January. The loan term is 10 month beginning in February. Interest of 6% is added at the beginning of the loan term and the equal monthly repayments include both capital and interest elements.

- When Yasmin uses its bank overdraft facility interest is payable monthly and is estimated at 2% of the previous months overdraft balance. The interest is to be rounded to the nearest £.

- Yasmin needs to buy some new camera equipment costing £3,000. She has negotiated to pay for this in equal instalments over 3 months starting in February.

- At 1 January the balance of the bank account was £5,750.

(e) **Using the information provided, complete the cash budget for Yasmin for the three months ending March.** (9 marks)

Cash inflows should be entered as positive figures and cash outflows as negative figures. Zeroes must be entered where appropriate to achieve full marks.

	January £	February £	March £
RECEIPTS			
Cash sales	720	760	840
Credit sales	1,080	1,128	1,116
Bank loan			
Total receipts			
PAYMENTS			
Purchases	−684	−722	−798
Wages	−110	−110	−110
Expenses	−2,200	−2,200	−2,200
Capital expenditure			
Bank loan repayment			
Overdraft interest			
Total payments			
Net cash flow			
Opening bank balance			
Closing bank balance			

TASK 3 (10 marks)

A cash budget has been prepared for J Blacktusk and Co for the next four periods.

The budget was prepared based on the following sales volumes and a selling price of £12 per item.

	Period 1	Period 2	Period 3	Period 4
Sales volume (items)	4,500	4,300	4,500	4,800

The pattern of cash receipts used in the budget assumed 20% of sales were received in the month of sale and the remaining 80% in the month following sale.

	Period 1 (£)	Period 2 (£)	Period 3 (£)	Period 4 (£)
Original forecast sales receipts	10,800	53,520	52,080	54,720

J Blacktusk and Co are now considering offering a settlement discount of 2% for all credit sales settled in the period of sale. The pattern of sales receipts changes to 60% of sales received in the month of sale, 20% in the month following sale and the remaining 20% two months after sale.

(a) Complete the table below to calculate the sales receipts expected in periods 1 to 4 (to the nearest £): (4 marks)

	Period 1 (£)	Period 2 (£)	Period 3 (£)	Period 4 (£)
Revised forecast sales receipts				

(b) Calculate how the revised receipts will affect the cash flow for Blacktusk and Co. (1 mark)

Blacktusk and Co will have £_____ more/less cash at the end of Period 4.

Blacktusk has a new supplier. The budgeted payments for the first month's purchases are shown below:

Month 1 (£)	Month 2 (£)	Month 3 (£)
14,250	6,000	2,000

J Blacktusk receive a 5% discount on any payments made in month 1.

(c) What are the total amount of purchases in month 1? (2 marks)

£ [   ]

(d) Select if the following are controllable or uncontrollable factors when adjusting the cash budget (3 marks)

	Controllable	Uncontrollable
Hot weather increasing demand of a product		
Change in interest rates		
Awarding a bonus to staff		

MOCK ASSESSMENT QUESTIONS : SECTION 3

TASK 4 (15 marks)

The quarterly budgeted and actual figures for J Blacktusk and Co are provided below. A variance of more than 7% is considered to be significant.

	Budgeted £	Actual £	Variance £
Credit sales	162,840	158,521	4,319 A
Cash sales	95,325	95,847	522 F
Total receipts	258,165	254,368	
Credit purchases	166,589	161,178	5,411 F
Cash purchases	10,520	10,875	355 A
Capital expenditure	12,000	20,000	8,000 A
Wages and salaries	45,000	40,000	5,000 F
General expenses	21,000	22,222	1,222 A
Total payments	255,109	254,275	
Net cash flow	3,056	93	

(i) Identify the significant variances and calculate the percentage change in these variances (2 marks)

(ii) Explain TWO potential reasons for each of these variances (4 marks)

(iii) Give ONE action that could be taken to rectify these variances and to reduce the likelihood of recurrence. (2 marks)

Significant variance and % change from budget	Possible reasons for variance	Potential corrective action

KAPLAN PUBLISHING

Significant variance and % change from budget	Possible reasons for variance	Potential corrective action

(b) Discuss the differences between overtrading and overcapitalisation (3 marks)

Mouse Ltd is a new business, specialising in computer set ups and repairs for small and medium size businesses. The owners of the business have taken out considerable business loans to help finance the initial capital expenditure. In order to attract customers, Mouse Ltd are offering long credit terms.

Business has grown quickly and profits are better than expected, but liquidity is suffering and Mouse Ltd is close to their agreed overdraft limit.

(c) Discuss the advantages of Mouse Ltd using cash budgets (4 marks)

AAT: CASH AND TREASURY MANAGEMENT

TASK 5 (15 marks)

(a) **Why is liquidity management important?** (1 mark)

- A Liquidity management is important to ensure that a company does not make a loss.
- B Liquidity management is important so that the shareholders can see how much return they will get on their investment.
- C Liquidity management is important so that the company can estimate how much cash is tied up in inventory and non-current assets.
- D Liquidity management is important so that the company can ensure that cash is available to discharge commitments.

(b) **Identify which statement describes a Government's fiscal policy, and which describes monetary policy** (2 marks)

	Fiscal policy	Monetary policy
Policies on tax and public spending		
Policies on tax rates and the supply of money		

(c) If a business decreases its receivable days by 8 days and increases the inventory holding period by 5 days and increased the time it takes to pay its payables by 12 days, what is the impact on the working capital cycle?

The working capital cycle would increase/decrease by ☐ days (1 mark)

(d) **Which TWO of the following are signs of overtrading?** (2 marks)

- A Rapidly decreasing sales
- B Rapidly increasing sales
- C Increased profit margins
- D Short receivables collection periods
- E Longer payables payment periods

(e) **Which TWO are part of the role of the treasury department in a trading company?** (2 marks)

	Tick
Invest surplus funds	
Raise finance	
Reduce the tax liability	
To speculate on risky investments	

(f) Tick if the following statements are true or false (4 marks)

	True	False
Under the Bribery Act is in an offence to accept money as a reward for performing a relevant function improperly		
Money laundering regulations cover accountants and solicitors		
Company Act is the legislation that governs anti-corruption measures		
If a UK company bribes an official in a country where bribery is not illegal, no criminal offence has occurred.		

Below are some extracts from the latest financial statements of Rad Ltd

Gross profit	£35,000
Operating profit	£24,000
Finance costs	£6,250
Share capital	£40,000
Retained earnings	£80,000
Long term liabilities	£15,000
Trade payables	£8,000

(g) Calculate the following ratios for Rad Ltd?

Interest cover is _____ times (2 decimal places) (1 mark)

Return of capital employed is _____ % (2 decimal places) (1 mark)

Gearing is _____ % (2 decimal places) (1 mark)

TASK 6 (10 marks)

(a) A bank has offered to lend a company £80,000 to be repaid over 40 months in equal instalments. The flat rate of interest is 3.75% per annum.

What is the monthly repayment of capital and interest to the nearest £? (1 mark)

£ [   ]

(b) **What is the annual flat rate of interest for a loan of £800,000 over 10 years if the monthly repayments are £16,000?** (1 mark)

[   ] %

(c) A company has arranged a bank overdraft facility of £40,000. It has the following terms:

- The current annual interest is 12.5%
- The interest is calculated on the closing monthly overdrawn balance and is included in the next month's opening balance
- Assume there are no differences in the monthly charges for the number of days in the month

Calculate the monthly interest costs to the nearest pound. Minus signs must be used to denote any bank overdraft and interest to be paid (4 marks)

AAT: CASH AND TREASURY MANAGEMENT

	Month 3	Month 4	Month 5
Forecast net cash flow	17,500	−17,500	25,000
Opening balance	−15,000		
Closing balance before interest			
Overdraft interest to be charged			

(d) **Identify if the following statement is true or false** (1 mark)

Statement	True	False
A lease does not affect the gearing of a company		

(e) **Which of the following best describes a capped rate of interest?** (1 mark)

  A   Interest rate that is guaranteed not to exceed a specified level

  B   Interest rate that remains the same for the period of borrowing

  C   Interest charge that floats in line with bank base rates

  D   Interest rate that fluctuates in line with an agreed indicator

(f) **Identify whether the following statements are true or false** (2 marks)

Statement	True	False
A fixed charge is security on a loan supplied by a group of assets		
A floating charge is security on a loan supplied by a specific asset		

TASK 7 (10 marks)

(a) A company has £1,000,000 to invest for 12 months.

The choices available are:

Option 1 – a deposit account offering interest paid at 2.5% each quarter

Option 2 – a deposit account offering interest at 10.25% per year, with interest paid annually

Which deposit account gives the best return? (1 mark)

	Tick
Option 1	
Option 2	

(b) **Calculate the interest yield (to 1 decimal places) on 4.5% Treasury Stock 20X4 with a current market price of £125.** (1 mark)

The interest yield is _____ %

(c) A company invests £35,000 in a 90 day notice period fixed interest deposit account for four years. The rate of interest is 7.5%.

What is the balance in the account after four years if the interest is paid annually at the end of each year and the interest received remains in the account (to 2 decimal places)?

£ _____ (1 mark)

MOCK ASSESSMENT QUESTIONS : SECTION 3

(d) A company invests £150,000 in shares of B Pearl, a quoted company. B Pearl has 2 million £1 shares in issue. The current market price of B Pearl's share is £1.25. B Pearl's operating profit in 20X3 was £0.7 million. The dividend paid to shareholders was 8p a share.

What is the dividend yield for B Pearl? (1 mark)

(e) **Identify whether the following statements are true or false** (4 marks)

	True	False
Government securities are considered a low risk investment		
Investing in land is considered to be a high risk investment		
When inflation rises, interest rates generally increase		
Gold is a type of commodity		

(f) A company has £576,000 invested in a one year fixed interest bond which pays 5% per annum. The company is going to have to withdraw the full amount from the investment in the 11th month of investment. The penalty for early redemption is the loss of one month's interest.

Calculate the total amount of interest that the company will receive. (2 marks)

TASK 8 (15 marks)

Oz Plc have £200,000 of surplus cash to invest. The finance director does not believe the cash will be required for at least three years and maybe longer. However it will certainly be required within five years.

(a) **Write a report which considers the risk, return and liquidity (including calculations) of the following investment options:** (12 marks)

- A piece of nearby undeveloped land. There is currently no building planning permission for the land but this could be applied for. If granted the land would rise significantly in value.

- Shares in another public company. The shares are currently priced at £2.50 per share and on average pay an annual dividend of 5p per share. The company is expected to grow significantly over the next few years. Oz plc would own less than 5% of the company.

- A four year fixed rate foreign bond with a coupon rate of 3% and trading at par

AAT: CASH AND TREASURY MANAGEMENT

1 Land

2 Shares in a public company

3 Foreign bond

(b) Identify THREE other factors that Oz Plc should consider before deciding which option to invest in (3 marks)

Section 4

ANSWERS TO MOCK ASSESSMENT QUESTIONS

TASK 1

(a)

Item	Cash	Profit	Cash and profit
Paying weekly staff wages			✓
Accrual for an expected telephone bill		✓	
Dividend payment to shareholders	✓		

(b) The cash paid was **£1,245**

Cash paid = opening accrual + expense − closing accrual = 275 + 1,350 − 380 = 1,245

(c)

	£
Operating profit	3,756
Change in trade receivables (decreased from 2,480 to 2,356)	+124
Depreciation	+1,000
Loss on disposal	+1,760
Net change in cash position	6,640

(d) **£175,000**

Cash paid = closing balance − opening balance + depreciation − revaluation = 475,000 − 285,000 + 25,000 − (150,000 − 110,000) = 175,000

TASK 2

(a) Index = (current price/base price) × 100. E.g. for 20X2: 41/34 × 100 = 120.6

Year	20X1	20X2	20X3
Price	34p	41p	45p
Index		120.6	132.4

(b) The forecast sales of pictures for Charlie and Sam's wedding is 17,600. This is calculated as 100 + (50 × 350).

(c) The adjusted forecast sales of pictures is 18,480. This is calculated as 17,600 from part a, plus 5% – 17600 × 1.05 = 18,480.

(d) The forecast selling price to achieve a 20% margin is £0.15 (to the nearest penny). Calculated as £0.12 × 100/80

The forecast selling price to achieve a 40% mark-up is £0.17 (to the nearest penny). Calculated as £0.12 × 140/100

(e)

	January £	February £	March £
RECEIPTS			
Cash sales	720	760	840
Credit sales	1,080	1,128	1,116
Bank loan	5,000	0	0
Total receipts	**6,800**	**1,888**	**1,956**
PAYMENTS			
Purchases	−684	−722	−798
Wages	−110	−110	−110
Expenses	−2,200	−2,200	−2,200
Capital expenditure – camera	0	−1,000	−1,000
Bank loan repayment – (5000 × 1.06) / 10 months	0	−530	−530
Overdraft interest	0	0	0
Total payments	**−2,994**	**−4,562**	**−4,638**
Net cash flow	**3,806**	**−2,674**	**−2,682**
Opening bank balance	5,750	9,556	6,882
Closing bank balance	9,556	6,882	4,200

TASK 3

(a)

	Period 1 (£)	Period 2 (£)	Period 3 (£)	Period 4 (£)
Period 1 sales	31,752	10,800	10,800	
Period 2 sales		30,341	10,320	10,320
Period 3 sales			31,752	10,800
Period 4 sales				33,869
Period 5 sales				
Revised forecast sales receipts	31,752	41,141	52,872	54,989

Example workings: Period 1 sales = 4,500 units × £12 = £54,000. In period 1, receive £54,000 × 60% 98% (discount) = £31,752. In periods 2 and 3, receive £54,000 × 20% = £10,800

(b) Blacktusk and Co will have £9,634 more cash at the end of Period 4

Working:

Original total receipts £171,120   Revised total receipts   £180,754

(c) **£23,000** = (14,250 × 100/95) + 6,000 + 2,000

(d)

	Controllable	Uncontrollable
Hot weather increasing demand of a product		✓
Change in interest rates		✓
Awarding a bonus to staff	✓	

ANSWERS TO MOCK ASSESSMENT QUESTIONS : SECTION 4

TASK 4

Significant variance and % change from budget	Possible reasons for variance	Potential corrective action
Capital expenditure (67% adverse)	Earlier expenditure may have been deferred to this period. Prices may have increased since the budget was set. The supplier may have reduced the availability of credit for capital purchases, hence need to pay in cash. More assets or higher specification assets may have been purchased.	This is a very large percentage variance but is not a large sum of money if you consider the overall receipts (£254,368) and payments (£254,275) that occur within the business. It does still need to be investigated as a serious overspend has occurred with regards capital expenditure. Future capital expenditure could be contracted for in advance with prices and payment terms agreed to avoid unexpected increases. Capital expenditure could be deferred to a later period to avoid an adverse variance.
Wages and salaries (11% favourable)	Less overtime may have been needed during the period. There may have been a reduction in staff due to natural wastage or leavers which has reduced the payroll costs for the period. The increase in capital expenditure may have been for machinery that has replaced employees.	If production levels have remained constant and have been accomplished without the need for overtime, then identify any changes in production processes that have enabled this and continue for the future. If the reduction is due to staff leaving which will need to be replaced then future budgets should not be reduced. If the reduction is due to redundancies as staff are no longer required this could lead to further costs in redundancy packages but the efficiency of the machinery should level out the costs in the long run.

KAPLAN PUBLISHING

AAT: CASH AND TREASURY MANAGEMENT

(b) Discuss the differences between overtrading and overcapitalisation

> Overtrading occurs when a business grows too quickly without sufficient working capital. This causes liquidity to suffer and the business to run out of cash.
>
> Overcapitalisation is when a business has too much working capital. This money is tied up in the business needlessly and would be better spent expanding the business or earning a better return elsewhere.

(c) Advantages of Mouse Ltd using cash budgets

> – Would help Mouse Ltd to identify if cash is available to meet loan repayments when due and to allow discussions with the bank in advance if they can not be met.
>
> – Can help Mouse Ltd monitor cash levels and reduce discretionary spending to stay within the overdraft limit.
>
> – Would allow Mouse Ltd to see the potential impact of reducing credit terms or offering an early settlement discount
>
> – Allows Mouse Ltd to identify if and when additional finance is required, or when extra capital expenditure could be afforded.

TASK 5

(a) **D**

(b)

	Fiscal policy	Monetary policy
Policies on tax and public spending	✓	
Policies on tax rates and the supply of money		✓

Fiscal policy refers to the government's taxation and spending policies. Monetary policy refers to the control of interest rates and monetary supply.

(c) The working capital cycle will **decrease by 15 days** – the decrease in the receivable days decreases the length of the cycle, the increase in inventory holding days increases the length of the cycle, the increase in the payment period decreases the length of the cycle – the net effect is a decrease of 15 days.

(d) **B and E**

(e)

	Tick
Invest surplus funds	✓
Raise finance	✓
Reduce the tax liability	
To speculate on risky investments	

(f)

Statement	True	False
Under the Bribery Act is in an offence to accept money as a reward for performing a relevant function improperly	✓	
Money laundering regulations cover accountants and solicitors	✓	
Company Act is the legislation that governs anti-corruption measures		✓
If a UK company bribes an official in a country where bribery is not illegal, no criminal offence has occurred.		✓

(g) **Interest cover is 3.84 times** (24,000 / 6,250)

Return on capital employed is 17.78% (24,000 / (40,000 + 80,000 + 15,000))

Gearing is 11.11% (15,000 / (40,000 + 80,000 + 15,000))

TASK 6

(a) **£2,250**

80,000 × 3.75% = £3,000 interest pa

£3,000 ÷ 12 × 40 = £10,000 total interest

(£80,000 + £10,000) ÷ 40 = £2,250

(b) **14%**

Total repayments = £16,000 × 12 × 10 = £1,920,000

Interest paid = £1,920,000 – £800,000 = £1,120,000

Interest rate = £1,120,000 ÷ £800,000 × 100 ÷ 10 years = 14%

(c)

	Month 3	Month 4	Month 5
Forecast net cash flow	17,500	–17,500	25,000
Opening balance	–15,000	2,500	–15,156
Closing balance before interest	2,500	–15,000	9,844
Overdraft interest to be charged	0	–156	0

(d)

Statement	True	False
A lease does not affect the gearing of a company		✓

A lease will increase the total debt of a company (due to the lease liability), increasing gearing.

(e) **A**

(f)

Statement	True	False
A fixed charge is security on a loan supplied by a group of assets		✓
A floating charge is security on a loan supplied by a specific asset		✓

TASK 7

(a)

	Tick
Option 1	✓
Option 2	

Option 1

The interest is 2.5% a quarter for 4 quarters.

£1,000,000 × 1.025 = £1,025,000

£1,025,000 × 1.025 = £1,050,625

£1,050,625 × 1.025 = £1,076,891

£1,076,891 × 1.025 = £1,103,813

Alternatively: 1 + APR = 1.025 ^ 4 = 1.1038. So APR = 0.1038 = 10.38%. This is higher than the annual 10.25% on option two.

Option 2

£1,000,000 × 1.1025 = £1,102,500

Therefore Option 1 gives the better return

(b) (£100 × 4.5%) ÷ 125 × 100 = 3.6%

(c) £35,000 × (1.075 ^ 4) = £46,741.42

(d) (8/125) × 100 = 6.4%

(e)

Statement	True	False
Government securities are considered a low risk investment	✓	
Investing in land is considered to be a high risk investment	✓	
When inflation rises, interest rates generally increase	✓	
Gold is a type of commodity	✓	

(f) £576,000 × 5% ÷ 12 × 10 = £24,000. Note only 10 months interest is earned due to the one month penalty.

TASK 8

Land

Risk

Land used to be considered as one of the most solid investments available as it will always be worth something, and there's little chance of it being stolen. However, in the last decade land values have been volatile, sometimes resulting in a capital loss for investors. There can be costly problems with getting planning permission. If permission is refused, then the land may fall in value. Therefore there is risk with regards the return available and also risk of losing the money invested, especially over (for land) a fairly short time period of 3-5 years.

Return

If planning permission is granted then land can be built on and sold or built on and rented out, increasing the value of the land. Purchase, maintenance and/or 'refurbishment' costs of the land can be high, reducing the possible profit on resale.

If planning permission is denied then it may be possible to rent the land as it is without development but this may reduce the value substantially.

If the market value is lower than the purchase price, at the date of sale, the initial investment may not be fully realised. It is unlikely that the return could be forecast with any certainty at the time of purchase.

It may be possible to rent it out to earn a return, but that will depend on the type and location of the land.

Liquidity

The investment can only be realised once the land is sold and the speed of this will depend upon the economic environment at the time of sale. It is often not a quick process and may be an issue if the money is needed urgently.

Shares

Risk

Shares in public companies are generally perceived to be high risk because of market volatility and lack of control over business decisions made by those running the company. The company could spread the risk by selecting a portfolio which includes both low risk and high risk companies. Shares are usually deemed to be more of a long term investment, but 3-5 years is a reasonable length of time to allow the shares to hopefully increase in value.

Return

When you buy shares in a company you own part of that company and will receive a share of any profits by way of dividends. Based on the current share price and expected dividend, these shares provide a dividend yield of just 2%, however the overall return may be far higher if the business grows and the share price rises

There are brokerage fees when shares are bought or sold, reducing the overall return, and share price fluctuation mean the return is uncertain. However, high returns can be achieved with the right portfolio of shares held for a reasonable period of time.

Liquidity

As shares can be sold at any point after purchase, it would take only a few days for the company to realise its cash, as long as it is prepared to take the price offered at that point in time. The company could also realise some of its cash as and when required.

Foreign bond

Risk

The fact that the bond is overseas makes this higher risk, since the returns and value may alter due to currency exchange rate fluctuations. The political stability of the country should also be considered, along with any potential foreign tax issues.

The bond is fixed rate so this protects Oz Plc, although the actual amounts received will vary if currency rates change.

Return

Assuming the currency rates don't change then the bond should earn annual interest of £6,000 (£200,000 × 3%) and the bonds may rise in price. There would be no benefit if interest rates rose, but if the home currency (pounds) weaken then the value of the investment and interest would rise

Liquidity

This is a five year bond and it is unknown if there is an active trading market where the bond could be sold if the money is needed before the expiry date.

(b) **Identify THREE other factors that Oz Plc should consider before deciding which option to invest in**

–	Alternative options such as UK bonds
–	If Oz could use the funds to repay any loans
–	If Oz has any potential opportunities to invest the money internally to grow the business (e.g. open up new branches, purchase more non-current assets, develop new products)
–	Any ethical issues with any of the investments (e.g. environmental damage by building on the land)
–	Risk attitude of directors and shareholders